# CONSTITUTIONAL CRISIS AND PROBLEMS IN INDIA

# CONSTITUTIONAL CRISIS AND PROBLEMS IN INDIA

Suchintya Bhattacharya

Publications

KALPAZ PUBLICATIONS

DELHI–110 052

**CONSTITUTIONAL CRISIS AND PROBLEMS IN INDIA**

(*Political Science*)

Rs. 540



ISBN: 81-7835-186-2



Published in 2003 in India by
Kalpaz Publications
C–30, Satyawati Nagar
Delhi–110 052
E-mail: Kalpaz@hotmail.com

*Lasertypesetting by:* Varsha Graphics, Delhi
*Printed at:* Mehra Offset Press, Delhi

*To*

*The Memory of My Parents*

**Surendra Nath Bhattacharya**

*and*

**Kalitara Devi**

# Contents

# Preface

The book, 'Constitutional Crisis and Problems in India' is an inquiry into the contemporary constitutional crisis in India with special reference to the on-going debates between those who argue that the present Westminster model of parliamentary democracy as most suited to India's experience and those who argue that Westminster system causes and abets destabilisation and criminalisation of politics.

As my analytical work proceeded, it became clear to me that the contemporary issue could not be seriously addressed in depth without looking at the broader dimensions of the overall historical background of the subcontinent. To begin with attempt has been made to introduce the political legacy in India. It was evident that anti-colonial freedom struggle was successful in creating an ideology and culture of democracy which finally led to the emergence of India as an independent nation and the path that India followed since independence had its deep roots in the political legacy of national movement.

The political features including the dominance of lawyers in the Constituent Assembly and especially in the drafting Committee, which account for legalistic character of the Indian constitution, have been presented in chapter II.

It is on the above background, a short historical survey of Constitutional development from the Councils Act of 1861 to the Government of India Act, 1935 which bears testimony to the fact that like any other constitution, Indian constitution is based on social, political and economic relevancy which constituted the philosophy of its own has been portrayed in chapter III. It is on this perspective an account of the crisis in Indian politics since independence has been dealt with in chapter IV. While dealing with the constitutional crisis, political evolution of the party system in various phases from 1947 till today have been analysed chronologically.

The fact reveals that parliamentary democracy and especially the coalition policy is a costly adventure in the present political system of India. The long mooted proposal of the present Westminster model's replacement by a new system of government installing a stronger and more effective executive against economic offenders committed to act independently of pressure groups or interest articulation have been treated in chapter V and chapter VI respectively.

The suitability of presidential type of government has been presented in chapter VII. This aspect has its importance because of the fact that United States of America is not the only country having presidential form of government but that there other countries like France, Finland, Switzerland, Egypt and Latin American democracies like Argentina, Brazil, Chile, Costa-Rica, Mexico, Uruguay and Venezuela where this system prevails. Besides, we have near at hand the country like Sri Lanka, Philippines, and Indonesia etc having presidential form of government.

The book tells that a new constitution for the aforesaid purpose is indeed a desideratum and in this respect, the framers of the constitution should rise above party politics and affiliations. Their consideration should be national interest only. Let the people who have not yet tasted the fruits of freedom decide this vital issue.

**Suchintya Bhattacharya**

# Acknowledgements

I must express my thanks and gratitude to Professor Diptendu Bhattacharya of Tripura Engineering College, Agartala, Tripura, India without whose help this book would not have been possible. He has helped me in checking the manuscript and made valuable suggestions.

I acknowledge my sincere feelings of gratitude to my teacher, Professor S.K. Choudhury, former of Principal, M.B.B. College, Agartala who took great pains to read the manuscript and also for making important suggestions.

I am grateful to my teacher, Professor J.B. Ganguly, former Vice Chancellor of Tripura University, Agartala. He has always been source of inspiration. This book is the result of his moral support and encouragement.

I am also grateful to Professor J.N. Clarke, Head of the Department of Political Science, the University of Arizona, Tucson, USA. She has helped me in procuring valuable materials of the American Presidency for the book.

I shall be failing in my duty, if I do not express my thanks to my wife Smt. Jayanti Bhattacharya, sons Sreeman Beacon and Sreeman Rupak, my daughters Suman and Sona and my grand daughter Rahel for their devotion that I hardly deserve.

I also express my thankfulness to the Kalpaz Publications, Delhi for co-operation in the completion of this book.

Finally, I will consider my labour amply rewarded if the book proves useful to those for whom it is intended.

**Suchintya Bhattacharya**

# 1
# The Political Legacy

Political systems of modern States are usually developments from earlier conditions. In India, the present structures and values of political system as well as the social and economic conditions which they operate are, also largely the products of British colonialism and the national movement. Empirical knowledge tells us that as a result of British rule, India was transformed by the end of the 19th century into a classic colony. It was a major market for British manufactures, a big source of raw materials and food stuffs and also an important field for the investment of British Capital.

The British brought about a most important transformation in India's agricultural economy. Of course, this was not with a view to improving Indian agriculture to increase production and ensure the welfare and prosperity of the Indians involved in agriculture, but to obtain for themselves in the form of land revenue all surplus available in agriculture and to force Indian agriculture to play its assigned role in a colonial economy. Old relationships and institutions were destroyed and new ones were imposed to extract the surplus available in agriculture. The colonial administration introduced the *Zamindari* and *Ryotwari* land revenue and tenurial systems. Subsequently, all these systems led to the emergence of a new structure of agrarian relations based on private property and also new social classes emerged with the landlords, intermediaries and moneylenders at the top and tenants at will, share croppers and agricultural labourers at the bottom.

According to the new *Zamindari* system which later on came to be known as *Mahalwari* system, old tax farmers, revenue collectors and *Zamindars* were turned into private landlords possessing some of the rights of private property in land and the bulk of the rent they derived from the tenants was supposed to be turned over to the Government. But however, under the *Ryotwari* system, the government itself collected revenues directly from the individual cultivators who were although, in law, recognised as the owners of the land; their right of ownership was limited by the temporary nature of the land revenue settlements. Now, because of the high revenue rates demanded and the rigid manner of collection, the peasant cultivator had to borrow money to pay taxes and not only that when his crops were ready he was invariably forced to sell his produce cheap or sell his property to the moneylender at a nominal price. In both the *Zamindari* and the *Ryotwari* areas there occurred a large-scale transfer of land from the hands of the actual cultivators to the hands of the moneylenders. In this regard, the whole administrative machinery helped the moneylenders because without him the collection of land revenue in time is, almost impossible. This new pattern of socio economic system was neither feudalism nor capitalism rather semi-feudal and semi-colonial in character.[1]

The growth of indebtedness and of the accompanying processes of mortgaging of lands and of sale and transfer of lands to non-agriculturists is responsible for acute agrarian crisis. Sir Edward Maclagan (1911) admitted: "The Writings of Munro, Elphinstone and others make it clear that there was much debt even at the beginning of our rule. But it is also acknowledged that the indebtedness has risen considerably during our rule, and more especially during the last half Century. The reports received from time to time and the evidence of annual sale and mortgage data show clearly there has been a very considerable increase of debt during the last half Century".[2] Carlyle compared the situation of British India with that of France on the eve the Great Revolution. He described the condition of the French peasantry in a famous passage: The widow is gathering nettles for her children's dinner: a perfumed seigneur, delicately lounging in the Oeil de Boeuf, has an alchemy, whereby he will extract from her the third nettle, and name it Rent and Law.[3]

The impact of the colonial rule on trade and industry was not less serious. Although foreign trade grew rapidly after 1858 increasing from Rs. 15 crores in 1834 to Rs. 60 crores in 1858 and reached a peak of Rs. 758 crores in 1924, the growth did not represent a positive feature in Indian economy. Because, it was used absolutely as the chief instrument through which the Indian economy was made colonial and dependent on world capitalism. The country was flooded with manufactured goods from Britain and forced to produce and export the raw materials Britain and other foreign countries needed.[4] Such policy only helped to transfer resources from peasants and crafts men to merchants, moneylenders and foreign capitalists.[5] It is significant to note that during this period there was constant excess of exports over imports but excess of exports did not represent the future claims of India on foreign countries, but the drain of India's wealth and resources.[6] One of the drastic consequences of British rule was the progressive decline and destruction of urban and rural handicraft industries. The ruin of the indigenous industries and the absence of other avenues of employment forced millions of craftsmen to crowd into agriculture and thereby pressure of population on land increased.

In support of this statement Sir Henry Cotton's observation (1890) will be representative in character. He says, "Less than a hundred years ago, the whole commerce of Dacca was estimated at one crore (ten millions) of rupees and its population at 200,000 souls. In 1787, the exports of Dacca muslin to England amounted to 30 lakhs (three millions) of rupees; in 1817 they had ceased altogether. The arts of spinning and weaving, which for ages afforded employment to a numerous and industrial population, have now become extinct. Families which were formerly in a state of affluence have been driven to desert the towns and betake themselves to the villages for a livelihood. This decadence has occurred not in Dacca only, but in all districts".[7] The same picture revealed in respect of the native iron-smelting industry has been practically stamped out by cheap imported iron and steel within range of railways, but it still persists in the more remote parts of the peninsula".[8]

In the words of K. Marx (1853): "From 1818 to 1836 the export of twist from Great Britain to India rose in the proportion of 1 to 5,200. In 1824 the export of British muslins to India hardly amounted to 6,000,000 yards, while in 1837 it surpassed 64,000,000 yards. But at the same time population of Dacca decreased from 150,000 inhabitants to 20,000. This decline of India town celebrated for their fabrics was by no means the worst consequence. British steam and science uprooted over the whole surface of Hindustan, the union between agricultural and manufacturing industry".[9]

Now, with the creation of a large labour force and a wide all India market with country wide transport system – the two basic requirements for the rise of a modern capitalists industry were fulfilled and thus paved the way for modern industries to appear gradually on Indians economic scene. Initially, that is, until the beginning of the twentieth century industrial development was mainly confined to four industries namely cotton and jute textile, coalmining and tea plantations and a few other minor industries like rice, flour, fibre etc.

But it was only during the First World War and the Great Depression of the 1930's that the Indian capitalist class found favourable condition because of lack of competition from foreign imports; the government was compelled to place large orders with Indian industrialists and merchants. However, India again entered into a period of stagnation under normal condition when colonial links were restored. On the whole the fact reveals that industrial development in India till 1947 was slow and stunted and did not at all represent an industrial revelation or even the initiation of one.

However, along with British rule a new economic and political life produced a deep impact on the social life of the Indian people. Modern industries, new means of transport, growing urbanisation and increasing employment of Women in factories offices, hospitals and educational institutions promoted social charge. Social exclusiveness and caste rigidities were eroded. The total disruption of old land and rural relationships upset the caste balance in the countryside. Besides, a link with the west, and modern ideas like rationalism and humanism which were first developed in Western Europe spread rapidly among the Indian people. These new ideas made them conscious about the socio-economic and political conditions and also to understand the nature of British imperialism in India which again in its turn facilitated the emergence of a powerful anti-colonial national movement in the late nineteenth century. The colonial government, however, did not remain passive. In order to meet the growing challenge of anti colonial national movement, the rulers followed the policy of divide and rule and actively encouraged communalism and castism which, in turn, strengthened the reactionary social forces.

Mention may be made that Lord William Bentinck, Governor General of India in an official speech during his term of office described with exemplary clearness the purpose of the permanent settlement as a bulwark against anti-colonial national movement. According to him: "If Security was wanting against extensive popular tumult or revolution, I should say that the permanent settlement, though a failure in many other respects and in most important essentials, has this great advantage at least, of having created a vast body of rich landed proprietors deeply interested in the continuance of the British Dominion and having complete command over the mass of the people".[10] A typical example may be cited in support of Bentinck's observation. In 1938, the first All-India Landholders' conference was held and the keynote of the Presidential address delivered by the Maharaja of Mymensingh, was to declare that "if we are to exist as a class then it is our duty to strengthen the hands of the Government".[11]

British writers and specially the colonists never failed to justify their political and economic domination over India. They declared that because of inherent social and cultural defects Indians were destined to be ruled perpetually by foreign masters. All these produced a strong reaction. Many Indians felt it necessary to prove their fitness for self-government by glorifying their remote past. Subsequently, freedom struggler under the leadership of Indian National Congress paved the way for emotional and psychological bond that knit the people together and led to the emergence of a common national outlook.[12]

The interesting point is that the official founder of the National Congress was an English administrator A.O. Hume, who after his retirement from government service took up the work of the formation of the Congress. Hume, in his official capacity had received some secret police reports which revealed the growth of popular discontent and the spreading of underground conspiratorial organisations. The disastrous famine of 1877 coinciding with costly durbar at which queen Victoria was proclaimed Empress of India and with the Second Afghan war unrest was met by repression. The freedom of the press was removed by the Vernacular Act of 1887 and in the following year the arms Act left the villagers without even the means of defence against the raids of wild animals.[13] The right of public meeting was cut down. All these ill-starred measures of reaction, combined with Russian methods of police repression brought India within measurable distance of revolutionary outbreak. Hume out of his own accord established contact with the Viceroy, Lord Dufferin in order to make clear to the authorities how almost desperate the situation had become. The new Viceroy, realising the gravity of the situation, encouraged Hume to go on with the formation of the Congress. The time was fully ripe for this all-India movement. In place of an agrarian revolt, which would have had the sympathy and support of the educated classes, it gave the rising classes a national platform from which to create a New India. It was all to the good in the long run that a revolutionary situation based on violence was not allowed to be created once again.[14] Hume's own conception of the role of the Congress may here be quoted, "A safety valve for the escape of great and growing forces, generated by our own action, was urgently needed and no more efficacious safety-valve than our Congress movement could possibly be devised".[15]

The calculation was perfectly clear. The aim was fulfilled. The first Congress was most dutiful to imperialism; its nine resolutions cover only derail administrative reform suggestions; the nearest approach to a national democratic demand was the request for the admission of some elected members to the legislative Councils. Thus, the twofold character of the National Congress is clear. On the one hand, the strand of co-operation with the imperialism against the 'menace' of the mass movement and on the other hand, the strand of leadership of the masses in the national struggle. This twofold character, which can be traced through all the contradictions of its leadership from Gokhale in the old stage to his disciple, Gandhi in the new, is the reflection of the twofold or vacillating role of the Indian bourgeoisie, at once, in conflict with the British bourgeoisie and desiring to lead the Indian people, yet fearing that too rapid advance may end in destroying its privileges along with those of the imperialists.[16] So they did not demand immediate fulfilment of the aspiration of self-government rather suggested a step-by-step approach towards freedom. For instance, they demanded the widening of the powers of the legislative councils and membership of the councils for the elected representatives of the people. Of course, such attitude is not without reason. The early Indian bourgeoisie understood very well that they were in no position to challenge British rule. So they thought that it would be wise to look to British rule as their ally. For them, the main enemy was not British rule as such, but the backwardness of the people, the lack of modern development of the country. In their fights against these evils they looked hopefully for the co-operation of the British rulers, but their faith and hope in British imperialism as their ally in this work were doomed to disappointment. British imperialism understood very clearly that the significance of this progressive role and the inevitable conflict that it would mean with the interests of the imperialist rule and exploitation. Therefore, from an early period the original patronage of the congress turned to suspicion and hostility. Within three years of its foundation, the viceroy, Lord Dufferin, its original inspirer, was speaking with contempt for the microscopic minority represented by the Congress.[17] In 1890, the Government issued a Circular forbidding Government officials to attend the Congress even as visitors. In 1900 Lord Curzon wrote in a letter to the Secretary of State: "The Congress is tottering to its fall, and one of my great ambitions while in India is to assist it to a peaceful demise".[18] As the failure of the old policy became clear, a new school associated especially with the leadership of B. G. Tilak came to the front, along with the other renowned lenders like Bipin Chandra Pal and Arabinda Ghosh of Bengal and Lajpat Ray of Punjab. The new school termed themselves nationalists and came to be widely known as 'Extremist' who made a great advance in their goal when they put forward the claim of Swaraj or Self government within the British empire on the model of self governing colonies like Australia and Canada. With the gradual widening of its social base the national movement acquired militancy during the Gandhian phase. During this phase 'Poorna Swaraj' or complete independence was made for the first time in 1929 in Lahore session of the Congress. It is important to note that although the definition of the nationalist political goal differenced in the Moderate, Extremist and Gandhian phases of the national movement, the goal of democratic self-government was implicit. In fact, the basic difference among them was not in goals but on how to realise them in practice. It is interesting to note that in spite of differences amongst them, in the national interest the moderates never failed to defend Tilak or Extremist or non-violent Gandhians never turned their faces against the revolutionary terrorists during their trials. Such posture, no doubt contributed a lot to the unifying force of democratic principles in the national movement.

In the 1930's, Indian national movement took a new turn. The Congress leadership began taking a more conscious interest in world affairs. During this time, Nehru as Indian representative attended the congress of oppressed nationalities at Brussels. The Conference was organised by political exiles and revolutionaries from Asian, African and Latin American countries where the people were suffering from economic or political exploitation by the imperialist powers. It was at this Congress Nehru declared, "We realised that there is much in common in the struggle which various subject and Semi-subject and oppressed people are caring on to-day. Their opponents are often the same, although they sometimes appear in different guises, and the means employed for their subjection are often similar".[19]

Thus, it seems that Congress openly supported national movements in the countries of Asia and Africa and at the same time gave unqualified support to antifascist struggles in Ethiopia, Spain and Czechoslovakia. Therefore, it is obvious that the above policy of the Indian National Congress was the outcome of recognition that the future of the countries of Asia and Africa were interlinked and that the approaching struggle between fascism and the forces of freedom, socialism and democracy would seriously affect India. Nehru did not fail to assign much importance to civil liberties and to give his ideas a concrete shape; the Indian Civil Liberation Union was formed out his imitative in 1936. Of course, from historical survey on defence of civil rights we come to know that from the beginning the politically conscious Indians had been attracted to modern civil rights, viz. the freedom of speech, the Press, thought and association. Reference may be made to the Vernacular Press act of 1878, which sought to gag Indian language newspapers, was firmly opposed by them till it was replaced in 1880. Similarly, official attempts during the 1890's to curb newspaper criticism under the garb of protecting official Secrets were stoutly opposed.[20] Another relevant incident in this respect was the arrest of B.G. Tilak and several other leaders and newspaper editors in 1897 on the charge of spreading disaffection against the government. Tilak, a stalwart of the nationalist movement was given rigorous imprisonment for 18 months. Besides, two Poona leaders, the Natu brothers, were deported without trial. Several other newspaper editors were meted out similar punishments. The nationalist newspapers and political associations were up in arms against this attack on civil liberties and a countrywide protest movement was organised. To add fuel to the fire, the government now enacted new laws to curb the freedom of speech and the Press and to increase the powers of the Police. As a result a nationwide opposition to these laws was organised.

It is evident that a new period of struggle, whih may prove decisive for the fate of British rule in India and for the future of the Indian people, is now opening. In relation to the problems of this present situation, a rapid survey may be taken of the previous stages of struggle and their lessons.[21]

The first wave of struggle was launched during the period from 1905-1910. At this stage, the maximum demand was representative institutions In support of this statement, Ramesh Chandra Dutt, President of the Congress in 1890, who formulated the demand of "the people of India" may be noted as follows: "The people of India are not fond of sudden changes and revolutions. They do not ask for new constitutions issuing like armed Minervas from the heads of legislative Jupiters. They prefer to work on lines, which have already been laid down. They desire to strengthen the present government, and to bring it more in touch with the people. They desire to see some Indian members in the Secretary of states council and in the Viceroy's Executive council, representing Indian agriculture and industries. They wish to see Indian members in an Executive Council for each province. They wish to represent interests of the Indian people in the discussion of every important administrative question. They seek that the administration of the Empire and its great provinces should be conducted with the co-operation of the people.[22]

There is a Legislative Council in each large Indian Province, and some of the members of these councils are elected under the act of 1892. The experiment has proved a success and some expansion of these Legislative Councils would strengthen administration and bring it more in touch with the people ..... A province with thirty districts and a population of thirty millions may fairly have thirty elected members on its Legislative Council. Each District should feel that it has some voice in the administrative of the Province.[23]

The above statement correctly reflected the position of the early Indian bourgeoisie. The Congress of those days was exclusively representative of the upper bourgeoisie, and especially of its ideological representatives, the educated middle class. While it won an enthusiastic and wide response from these circles from the outset, so much so that measures had to be taken from an early date to restrict the number of delegates, that response was entirely confined to these social elements.[24] It is interesting to note that an English Member of the Parliament W. S. Caine who attended the 1889

Congress wrote: "The four thousand gentleman sitting round me are picked men of the legal, medical, engineering and literary profession all over the world".[25]

The early moderate leaders were well aware that they did not represent the masses, and that while they might endeavour to speak as interpreters in the name of the people.

The fact cannot be denied that the Indian bourgeoisie of that time understood very well that they were in no position to challenge British rule. On the contrary, they looked to British rule as their ally. For them the main enemy was not British rule as such, but backwardness of the people, the lack of modern development of the country, the strength of the forces of obscurantism and ignorance and the administrative sortcomings of the bureaucratic system responsible for the situation. In their fight against these evils they looked hopefully for the co-operation of the British rulers.[26]

It is interesting to note the declaration of Ananda Mohan Bose, President of 1898 Congress. He says, "the educated classes are the friends and not the foes of England – her natural and allies in the great work that lies before her."[27]

The above statements, however, do not suggest that the early Congress leaders were reactionary and anti-nationals; on the contrary, they represented at that time the most progressive force in Indian society. But this policy was not only vicious in principle but also mistaken in tactics. It not only inevitably weakened the advance of the political consciousness and clarity of the movement but also divided the advancing forces. In the practical struggle the orthodox nationalists, while building on this religious basis for their argument, could derive no weapon or plan of action there from save the universal weapon of desperate but impotent, petty bourgeoisie elements divorced from any mass movement. Even here the fruits of the very vague general religious incitation and exaltation, and formation of secret societies were very meagre and played no part of importance until later the ripening of the situation for a new stage of struggle brought also these aspect to the front as an accompaniment.[28]

The second great wave of struggle took off during the period 1919-1922. In fact, it was the shock of the First World War with its lasting blow to the whole structure of imperialism and the opening of the world revolutionary wave that followed in 1917 and after which released the first mass movement of revolt in India. Reference may be made that the War of 1914 following the lesson of the defeat of Russian Tsarist by Japan a decade earlier, completed the shattering of the myth of the invincibility of western imperialism in the eyes of the Asiatic peoples. Palme Dutt (1940) rightly observed, "The spactacle of the suicidal conflict of the imperialist power aroused hapes in the breasts of millions of the subject peoples that the hour of collapse of the existing empires was at hand".[29] Without sparing much time the imperialist power also took firm measure from the outset to hold the situation in hand by the adoption of special legislation and powers, notably the Defence of India Act and by the imprisonment or internment of the most irreconcilable fighters or members of the revolutionary groups. In this task, it was assisted in the earlier period of the imperialist war by the willing co-operation of the upper sections of the political movement. The Congress, under the control of the moderate leaders proclaimed its loyalty and support of the imperialist war in revolutions adopted at each of its four annual sessions during the war. But in spite of the docility of the upper political leadership, the growth of mass unrest from the conditions of the war could not be checked. The growing unrest began to find a reflection in the political movement in which new stirrings appeared from 1916 onwards. In 1916 Tilak founded the Home Rule League. Interestingly the English theosophist Mrs. Besant who sought to guide the national movement in channels of "loyalty" joined his campaign to the empire and was later to take an active part in the fight against non-co-operation. Reunion between the extremists and moderates was achieved at the Lucknow Congress in 1916. Even more important, the plans for the Moslem League which had been originally prepared at the Karachi Congress in 1913 reached fruition in 1916. It is important to note that one of the reason for this closer understanding was that Muslim feeling had been strongly aroused by the war against Turkey and the Muslim League conference of 1915 had already revealed this content. Subsequently, in 1919 the Congress decided for working the reforms and Gandhi urged the task of the national movement was "to settle down quietly to work so as to make them a success. But the situation left no room for such dreams to be realised. The revolutionary tide of rising mass unrest, which had swept forward in 1919 was still advancing in 1920 and 1921 and was to be further intensified by the economic crisis which began to develop in the later part of 1920. It was in this situation Gandhi and the main body of Congress leadership executed a decisive change of front, threw over co-operation with the reforms determined to take the leadership of the rising mass movement, and for this purpose evolved the plan of non-violent non-co-operation. The new programme was finally adopted at the annual session of the congress at Nagpur in December 1920. The creed of the Congress was changed from the previous proclamation of the aim of colonial self-government within the empire, to be attained by constitutional means to the new aim of "attainment of swaraj by peaceful and legislative means".[30] The organisation of the congress was carried forward from its previous loose character to the machinery of the modern party with its units reaching down to the villages and localities and with a standing Executive Committee".[30]

But Gandhi's plan of campaign was less clear than the date of victory. In this context, Jawharlal Nehru writes of the "delightful vagueness" of Gandhi. He says, "It was obvious that to most of our leaders swaraj meant something much less than independence. Gandhiji was delightfully vague on the subject and he did not encourage clear thinking about it either".[31] Subhas Bose also relates his disheartenment. He remarked, "what his real expectation was, I was unable to understand. Either he did not want to give out all his secrets prematurely or he did not have a clear conception of the tactics whereby the hands of the government could be forced.[32]

However, the new factor which developed for the first time in the middle of the nineteen twenties may be regarded as the third great wave of struggle of 1930-1934. It gave the decisive impetus to the new wave of struggle, though not its leadership was the emergence of the industrial working class as an independent force, conducting its own struggle with unexampled energy and heroism and beginning to develop its own leadership. With this advance the new ideology of the working class or socialism began to develop for the first time as a political factor in India and the influence of its ideas began to penetrate the youth and the left sections of Indian nationalism, bringing new life and energy and wider horizons.

It is thus evident anti-colonial freedom struggle, was successful in creating an ideology and culture of democracy which finally led to the emergence of India as an independent nation and the path that India followed since independence had its deep roots in the Political legacy of national movement. In fact, people learnt the values of parliamentary democracy under the British rule. The liberal of the

Congress appreciated British sense of justice and supported introduction of the system of responsible government in India as prevailing in England.

## References


1. *Chandra Bipan*, Tripathi Amales, De Barun: Freedom struggle, National Book Trust, India New Delhi, 1982.
2. The Report of the Central Banking Enquiry committee, 1931 p. 55; Datta, R.P. Indians To-day, Calcutta.
3. Dutt, R. Palme: India To-day p. 257 Calcutta.
4. Chandra Bipan etc.: Freedom Struggle p. 20.
5. *Ibid.*
6. *Ibid.*
7. Dutt, R. Palme: India To-day p. 120.
8. Imperial Gazetteer of India, 1907 Vol. III p. 145.
9. Marx, K: The British rule in India New York Daily Tribune, June 10, 1853 India To-day, p. 89-90.
10. Lord William Bentinck: Speech on November 8, 1829 reprinted in A.B. Keith, speeches and Documents on Indian policy 1750-1921 Vol. I P. 215; India To-day, p. 233.
11. *Ibid.*
12. *Ibid.*
13. *Ibid.*
14. Andrews and Mukherjee: Rise and Growth of the Congress in India pp. 128-129; India To-day, p. 315.
15. Sir William Wedderburn: Allon Octovian Hume, Father of the Indian National Congress 1913, India To-day, p. 317.
16. Dutt, R. Palme: India To-day, pp. 317-318.
17. *Ibid.*, p. 323.
18. Ronaldshay; Life of Lord Curzon "Vol. II p. 51 India To-day, p. 323.
19. Chandra Bipan etc: Freedom stuggle p. 204.
20. Johari, J.C., New Delhi, 1996 Third Revised and Enlarged Edition, 2000 p. 21.
21. Dutt. R. Palme: India To-day, p. 321.
22. Dutt R. C.: The Economic History of India, Vol. I, p. XVIII.
23. *Ibid.*

24. Dutt. R. Palme: India To-day p. 321.
25. *Ibid.*
26. *Ibid.*, p. 322.
27. *Ibid.*
28. *Ibid.*
29. *Ibid.*
30. *Ibid.*
31. Nehru Jawaharlal: Autobiography p. 76.
32. Bose, Subhas: The Indian Struggle 1920-1934 p. 68.

# 2

# The Making of the Constitution

Modern scholars are of the opinion that the real constitution is the actual relations of power in a given society. Probably nowhere is this more clearly demonstrated than over the question of the Indian constitution. The various 'constitutions' or constitutional projects of imperialism for India were not solutions or even attempted solutions of the Indian problem. They were simply forms of the battle, successive stages and arenas of the battle between imperialism and nationalism. They were not even the main stage of the battle. The reality was the battle; the ghost was the constitution.[1] This view will be evident from Macaulay's observation (1833). He says: "In India you cannot have representative institutions. Of all the innumerable speculators who have offered their suggestions on Indian politics not a single one, as far as I know, however, democratically his opinion, has ever maintained the possibility of giving at the present time such institutions to India".[2]

It is important to note that John Stuart Mill, the accredited prophet of philosophic liberalism and champion of representative institutions, was no less emphatic in denying such institutions to India. In the same speech Macaulay quoted Mill's view: "He (Mill) has written strongly – far too strongly, I think – in favour of pure democracy... But when he was asked before the committee of last year whether he thought representative government practicable in India, his answer was: Utterly out of question".[3]

Mention may be made in this context an interesting dialogue between Gladstone and Bright illustrates the bankruptcy of nineteenth century liberalism before the problems of India" "I have had a very long conversation with Bright this evening on India........ He admits the difficulty of governing a people by a people, i.e., India by a pure Parliamentary Government".[4]

As regards the standpoint of British imperialism it may further be added that on the eve of first world war this was expressed in emphatic terms by Lord Cromer (1910): "To speak of self-government for India under conditions such as these as if were to advocate self-government for a united Europe... The idea is not only absurd; it is not only impracticable. I would go further and say that to entertain it would be a crime against civilisation and especially against the voiceless millions in India whose interests are committed to our charge".[5]

Again, no less definite was the expression of Liberal Lord Morley in the same period, which while introducing the constitutional reforms known as the Morley-Minto reforms was most insistent that they should not be regarded as in any sense preparing the way for parliamentary institutions. Lord Morley (1908) remarks: "If it could be said that this chapter of reforms led directly or indirectly to the establishment of a parliamentary system in India. I, therefore, would have nothing at all to do with it".[6]

Lord Morley's calculations to defeat the movement for self-government by his reforms were openly expressed. He analysed the situation in this way: There are three classes of people whom we have to consider in dealing with a scheme of this kind. These are the extremists who nurse fantastic dreams that someday they will drive us out of India. The second group nourish no hopes of this sort, but hope for autonomy or self-government of the colonial species and pattern. And then the third section of this classification asks for no more than to be admitted to co-operation in our administration".[7] He added, "I believe the effect of the reforms has been, is being and will be to draw the second class, who hope for colonial autonomy, into the third class, who will be content with being admitted to a fair and full cooperation".[8]

Thus 'co-operation in our administration', along with the path of constitutional reforms, was the chosen method of imperialism by which it hoped to defeat the national aim of self-government.

The situation, however, changed in 1914 when First World War commenced. The weakening of the foundations of imperialism, the awakening of India, as of all the colonial peoples, Hindu-Muslim unity and Congress-League scheme of 1916 for self-government and moreover the Russian revolution of 1917, opened the wave of popular advance in all countries. To combat the situation, the British government on August 20 1917, the British government met this situation with a new declaration of policy, which has since been regarded as the keystone of modern imperialist constitutional policy.

It is with a view to prepare a scheme of reforms Montague came to India in 1917. He met the Indian leaders and tried to understand their aspirations. In consultation with the governor general Lord Chelmsford he prepared 'The Report on Constitutional Reforms' which came to be known as 'Montford Report'. It was published in July 1918 and became the basis for the Government of India act, 1919. But the Extremists who then dominated the Congress did not favourably receive the Montague-Chelmsford Report. Annie Besant described it as "unworthy to be offered by England or to be accepted by India". A special session of the Congress, held at Bombay in August 1918 denounced the Montague-Chelmsford Report as, inadequate, unsatisfactory and disappointing.[9] It is interesting to note that at the outset Mahatma Gandhi himself welcomed the act of 1919 and not only that he in his speech to the Amritsar session of the Congress on 1st January 1920 urged the Congress to grasp the extended hand of the king emperor and take the fullest advantage of the Reforms.[10] And Congress also at his instance adopted a resolution offering its thanks to Mr. E.S. Montague for his labour in connection with the reforms. But just eight months later in the Calcutta session held on 8th September 1920 Gandhiji gave a contradictory statement. He said, "I come to the final point, namely boycott of councils. I must confess that I have not yet heard of a single argument in favour of going to councils".[11]

Subsequently Mahatma Gandhi placed a demand to the British Government in 1922, that Indians themselves should determine India's political destiny only. The Joint Parliamentary Committee immediately rejected the demand on the ground that "a specific grant of constituent powers to authorities in India is not at the moment a practicable proposition".[12] Lloyd George, as Prime Minister in his famous 'Steel frame' speech in the House of Commons gave a proud reply to Gandhiji's proposition stating that Britain under no Circumstances will relinquish her responsibility in India as a cardinal principle, not merely of the present Government but of any government which will command the confidence of the people in this country.[13] Winston Churchill sharing the view of Lloyd George declared in 1930. "The British nation has no intention whatever of relinquishing effectual control of Indians life and progress. We have no intention of casting away that most truly bright and precious jewel in the crown of the king, which more than all our other Dominions and Dependencies constitute the glory and strength of the British Empire".[14]

In the background of such basic imperialist policy, A National Conference was held in New Delhi on February 12 and 13 of 1923 for purposes of making arrangements for the calling of the National Convention after the elections of 1923 but the idea did not take a real shape. The newly formed Swaraj Party in the central legislature put forward in the legislative Assembly a demand for the Round Table Conference or Convention for recommending a scheme of Constitution for India. This demand was reiterated in 1925 when the report of the Muddiman Committee was being discussed and considered in the Central Legislative Assembly. It was true that the demand of the Swaraj Party was not analogous to that of a Constituent Assembly, but however, the germs were there.

It is unfortunate that the colonial attitude of the British Government in appointing andall white' purely Parliamentary Commission, under the chairmanship of Sir John Simon, in 1927, was an open challenge to the patriotism of the Indians. Naturally, national leaders and vast bulk of the politically minded people boycotted the commission. Historical record reveals that it was at this stage that Sri M. N. Roy put forward, for the first time, the idea of a Constituent Assembly for India. But Roy's suggestion was not accepted till 1930 when the congress declared in January, full independence as India's goal but no mention was made about the constituent Assembly. The Resolution of the working committee simply declared: "We believe therefore, that India must sever the British Connection, and attain 'Purna Swaraj' or complete independence.[15]

In fact, the demand for a constituent Assembly entered Indian politics in 1934. Mention may be made that on April 7, 1934, Mahatma Gandhi approved the proposal to revive the Swaraj Party. The Swaraj Party was formed at Ranchi in the same year and it placed before the country a programme which inter alias claimed for India, in common with other nations, the right of self-determination and maintained that "the only method of applying that principle is to convene a constituent Assembly representative of all sections of the Indian people to frame an acceptable constitution".[16] "The policy of the Swaraj Party was approved by the All India Congress Committee at its Patna session on the 18th and 19th May, 1934. The demand for the constituent Assembly from that time on became the platform of the congress. As regards the meaning and significance of the demand for the constituent Assembly, it was embodied in the famous resolution passed by the Indian National congress at its Faizpur Session on December 28, 1936 that the congress stands for a genuine democratic state in India where political power has been transferred to the people as a whole and the Government is under their effective control. Such a state can only come into existence through a constituent Assembly elected by adult suffrage and having the power to determine finally the constitution of the country".[17] Subsequently, however, the demand for a Constituent Assembly was ratified by passing resolutions in the provincial Legislative Assembly in which the congress ratified Assembly commanded majority. Again, in November, 1939, after the declaration of world war, the working committee of the congress reiterated its demand through resolution stating, "wish to declare again that recognition of India's independence and the right of her people to frame their constitution is essential in order to remove the taint of imperialism from Britain's policy and to enable the congress to consider further cooperation. They hold that the constituent Assembly is the only democratic method of determining the constitution of a free country, and no one who believed in democracy and freedom can possibly take exception to it. The working committee believed that the constituent Assembly is the not only adequate instrument for solving command and other difficulties".[18] Interestingly, many were sceptical about the political efficacy. As for example, the Indian liberals opposed it because they thought the people of India were not politically equipped to realise its significance. The princess, the Europeans, the landlords and other vested interests were opposed to it as they were afraid that their privileged position might disappear. Muslim league was also against the formation of an Indian Constituent Assembly as they were afraid that their special rights and interests would not be considered. Mention may be made in this context that during the late 1920s and

1930s, the disagreement; between; the Hindus and the Muslims had led to great communal tension. The leader of the Muslim League, Mr. M.A. Jinnah declared that the "Muslims are culturally as well as religiously a distinct group. They are neither Hindus nor Indians. They can only seek fulfilment in a separate state".[19] Accordingly, after the Lahore Resolution on Pakistan in March 1940, the Muslim League adopted a favourable attitude towards the idea of the Constituent Assembly only on the condition that two separate Constituent Assemblies are to be formed, one for Pakistan and the other for Hindustan. But the congress leaders did not agree with this view. They argued that the people of India were basically Indians, no matter what their religion. The Britain should; first leave the country and only then Indians could come together and settle their own differences by way of mutual discussion. The demand for the Constituent Assembly was however resisted by the British Government till the outbreak of the World War II when the pressure of external circumstances forced them to realise the urgency of solving the Indian constitutional problem. In March 1942, when Japanese were at the door of India, the British Government sent Sir Stafford Cripps, a member of the cabinet, with a draft declaration of the proposals of the government which were to be adopted provided the two major political parties—Congress and Muslim League could come to an agreement to accept them.[20]

The draft declaration of the proposals was as follows:[21]

(i) Immediately upon cessation of hostilities, steps shall be taken to set up in India in manner described hereafter an elected body charged with the task of framing a new constitution for India.

(ii) Provision shall be made for participation of Indian states in the constitution making body.

(iii) His Majesty's Government undertake to accept and implement forthwith the constitution so framed subject only to

(a) the right of any province of British India that is not prepared to accept the new constitution to retain its present constitutional position, provision being made for its subsequent accession if it so decides. With such non-acceding provinces, should they so desire, his Majesty's Government will be prepared to agree upon a new constitution giving them the same full status as the Indian Union and arrived at by a procedure analogous to that here laid down.

(b) The signing of a treaty, which shall be negotiated between His Majesty's Government, and the constitution making body. This treaty will cover all necessary matters arising out of the complete transfer of responsibility from British to Indian hands; it will make provision, in accordance with undertakings given by His Majesty's Government for the Protection of racial and religious minorities; but will not impose any restriction on the power of the Indian Union to decide in future its relationship with other member states of the British commonwealth. It will be necessary to negotiate a revision of its treaty arrangements so far as this may be required in the new situation, whether or not an Indian state elects to adhere to the constitution.

(iv) The constitution-making body shall be composed as follows unless the leaders of Indian opinion in the principal communities agree upon some other form before the end of hostilities. Immediately upon the result being known of provincial elections, which will be necessary at the end of hostilities, the entire membership of the lower houses of Provincial legislatures shall as a single electoral college proceed to the election of the constitution making body by the system of proportional representation. This new body shall be in number about 1/10th of the number of the Electoral College. Indian states shall be invited to appoint representatives in the same proportion as to their total population as in the case of representatives of British India as a whole and with the same powers as British Indian members.

(v) During the critical period which now faces India and until the new constitution can be framed his Majesty's Government must inevitably bear the responsibility for and retain the control and direction of the Defence of India as part of their world war effort but the task of organising to the full the military, moral and material resources of India must be the responsibility of the Government of India with the Co-operation of the peoples of India His Majesty's Government desire and invite the immediate and effective participation of the leaders of the principal sections of the Indian people in the counsels of their country, of the commonwealth and of the united nations. Thus, they will be enabled to give their active and constructive help in the discharge of a task, which is vital and essential for the future freedom of India.

The Draft Declaration was rejected by almost all the parties, though for different and diametrically opposite reasons. The congrèss did not welcome the principle of non-accession for any province. The working committee observed, "the committee cannot think in terms of compelling the people of any territorial unit to remain in all Indian Union against their declared and established will".[22] The Congress also found the introduction of non-representative elements in the Constituent Assembly is unacceptable. But most of all did not want to rely on future promises.

The Muslim league, although welcomed the possibility of provinces remaining outside the union, because of the recognition implicit in it that the Muslim majority provinces and areas may, if they so desired, form a separate union of their own but the league rejected the proposals on the ground that the procedure envisaged for the drafting of a "constitution was vague and the offer itself was rigid and did not permit of any modifications".[23] The Hindu Mahasabha feared partition of the country and therefore apposed the proposals. "The Sikh communalists did not favour because they were afraid that the Muslim majority of the Punjab would apt to stay out of the Union. Dr. Ambedkar also rejected the proposal on the ground that the *Harijans* would be left at the mercy of caste Hindus".[24] Thus, ultimately the proposals were rejected and the Cripps Mission failed to resolve the deadlock.

After rejection of the Cripps proposal, attempts however, were being made to reconcile the two parties and these again having failed; the British Cabinet sent three of its own members including Sir Stafford Cripps himself, to make another serious attempt with some altered proposals which were announced simultaneously in India and in England on the 16th May, 1946.

It is important to note that the scheme laid down by the cabinet Mission, was however, recommendatory in nature and it was contemplated by the Mission that if would be adopted by agreement between the two major parties viz., Congress and Muslim league.

**The New Constitutional proposals of 1946**

(1) There should be a Union of India embodying both British India and the States, which should deal with Foreign Affairs, Defence and communications and should have the poser necessary to raise

the finance required for these subjects.

(2) The Union should be an executive and legislature constituted from British Indian and State representatives. Any question raising a major communal issue in the legislature should require for its decision a majority of the representatives present and voting of each of the two major communities (Congress and Muslim League) as well as a majority of all members present and voting.

(3) All subjects other than Union subjects and all residuary powers should vest in the Provinces.

(4) The States should retain all subjects and powers other than those ceded to the union.

(5) The provinces should be free to form Groups, with Executives and Legislatures and each Group could determine the Provincial subjects to be taken in common.

(6) The constitutions of the Union and of the Groups should contain a provision whereby any province could, by majority vote of its legislative Assembly, call for a reconsideration of the terms of the constitution after an initial period of ten years and at ten yearly intervals thereafter.

Besides, the above recommendations for the future constitution the commission put forwarded the following proposals for constitution making machinery. These are:[25]

(i) A constituent Assembly of 389 members, 292 from the provinces of British India indirectly elected on a communal basis with separate seats allotted according to population for general, Muslim and Sikh groupings by the existing Provincial legislative Assemblies: and 93 from the states, the method of selection to be arranged by consultation.

(ii) Division of Provinces in three sections:

(a) Representing the Hindu majority regions (Madras, Bombay, United Provinces, Bihar, Central Provinces and Orissa).

(b) Representing the North Western Muslim majority region (Punjab, North-West Frontier Province, Sind and Baluchistan) and another representing the North-eastern Muslim majority region (Bengal and Assam) Representatives of these Groups to meet separately to determine the provincial constitutions for the provinces in each Group. The provinces to have the right to opt out only after the completion of the new constitution and the first elections on this basis.

(iii) Advisory committee for smaller minorities.

(iv) Union constituent Assembly to determine the union constitution.

Resolutions were raising major communal issues to require a majority of the representatives present and voting of each of the two major unities.

If is clear from the above proposals that the cabinet Mission rejected the claim for a separate Constituent Assembly and a separate State for the Muslims, the Scheme which they recommended involved a virtual acceptance of the Principle of the claim of the Muslim league by grouping the provinces on the lines suggested by the Muslim and giving the centre narrow and embayed powers relating to there subject only viz. Foreign Affairs, Defence and Communications.[26]

It is, however, interesting to note that a curious situation arose after an election for forming the constituent Assembly was held. The Muslim league joined this election and its candidates were returned. But a difference of opinion had in the meantime arisen between the congress and the league regarding the interpretation of the grouping clauses of the proposals of the cabinet Mission.[27] The British Government intervening the situation explained that they upheld the contention of the league as correct and on 6th December 1946 declared that should a constitution come to be framed by the constituent Assembly in which a large section of the Indian Population had not been represented. His Majesty's Government would not contemplate forcing such a constitution upon any unwilling part of the country.[28]

Henceforth, for the first time, the British Government acknowledged the possibility of two constituent Assemblies and two states. As a result, on 9th December 1946, when the constituent Assembly first met, the Muslim League members did not attend and it began to function with the non-Muslim members only. The Muslim League next urged the dissolution of the Constituent Assembly of India on the ground that it was not fully representative of all sections of the people of India. The British Government again declared on

20th February 1947 that the British rule in India would in any case end by June, 1948 after which the British would certainly transfer authority to Indian hands and if a fully representative constituent Assembly failed to work out a constitution. In accordance with the proposals made by the Cabinet Delegation His Majesty's Government will have to consider to whom the powers of the central Government in British India should be handed over, on the due date, whether as a whole to some form of central Government for British India, or in some areas to the existing Provincial Governments or in such other way as seem most reasonable and in the best interests of the Indian people.[29] The result was quite obvious. The Muslim league did not consider it necessary to join this Assembly and went on pressing for separate constituent Assembly for the Muslim population of India. The British Government next sent Lord Mountbatten to India as the Governor General, in place of Lord Wavell, in order to expedite the preparations for the transfer of power, for which they had fixed a rigid time limit. On 3rd June 1947 Lord Mountbatten announced that on 15th August 1947 British Government would recognise the existence of two states — India and Pakistan. The Indian independence Act passed by the British Government came into force on 15th August 1947. It formally gave legal status to the Constituent Assembly. The Cabinet Mission plan became outdated and the Constituent assembly settled down to draft India's constitution.

The main provisions of the Indian independence act, 1947 were:

1 Two dominions were constituted – India and Pakistan.

2 The king would appoint a Governor General for each domain.

3 The legislatures of each domain would have sovereign powers to legislate. No legislation passed by the British Parliament would apply to the Domains.

4 Governor General would have full power to assent to any bill in the name of His Majesty.

5 The suzerainty of his majesty over the Indian states would lapse.

6 Until a new constitution is framed the act of 1935 was to be taken as the constitution (subject to adaptation and modifications).

7 The constituent assembly would have no limitation on its powers.

8 The constituent assembly would function as the legislative assembly for the interim period.

Scholars are however, of the opinion that the granting of independence was not out of romantic idea. As a matter of fact circumstances forced the British imperialists to grant independence to India. Mention may be made that the anti British riots of 1942 during Quit India Movement. The INA under Subhas Chandra Bose fighting on the side of Japan, Indian navy mutiny of 1946 and other violent trends and open assertion of disaffection towards the British were the pointers that if the British resisted the national awakening they would be liquidated by an armed revolution.[31]

It is significant to note that the constituent assembly elected for undivided India, which had met for the first time on 9th December 1946, was convened to meet on 14th August 1947 and became the sovereign constituent assembly for divided India now called the domain of India. Members representing Bengal, Punjab, Sind, NWFP, etc. ceased to be members of the constituent assembly. In the process Dr. B.R. Ambedkar who had been elected from Bengal lost his seat. He was later elected by Bombay legislative congress party.[32] Whereas the Muslim league had joined the interim government but abstained from sending its representative to the constituent assembly, which was an integral part of the cabinet plan. Nehru moved the objective resolution on the 9th December 1946. On the advice of Dr. Jayakar and Dr. Ambedkar the assembly waited for long six weeks before passing the resolution on 22nd January 1947 for the Muslim League and representatives of Indian states to join.[33]

The constitutional advisor to the assembly Sir B. N. Rao prepared a draft constitution in October 1947. It contained 243 articles and 13 schedules. A drafting committee was elected by the constituent assembly on 29th August of the same year. It elected Dr. B. R. Ambedkar to be its President. The constitution as prepared by the drafting committee was circulated on 21st February 1948. This formed the basis of discussion in and outside the constituent assembly. It contained 315 articles and 8 scholars and was introduced on November 4 1948 by Dr. Ambedkar. The total number of amendments to the draft constitution tabled was 7,635 while 2,473 amendments were actually moved in the assembly.[34]

As regards elections to the constituent assembly mention may be made that the constituent assembly was elected by indirect election by the members of the provincial legislative assemblies under a scheme formulated by the cabinet mission. The main feature of the scheme were:[35]

(i) Each province and Indian state or group of states in case of small states were allotted seats in proportion to their respective population. One seat was allotted for a million approximately and as a result the provinces were to elect 292 members and the princely states were given a minimum of 93 seats.

(ii) Seats in each province were distributed among the communities Muslim, Sikh and general in proportion to their population.

(iii) Members of each community in the provincial assemblies elected their representatives by the method of proportional representation by single transferable vote.

(iv) The method of selection in the case of Indian states was to be determined by the constitution. In fact, it was mostly by nomination by the ruler.

Finally under the plan of 3rd June 1947 a separate constituent assembly was set up for Pakistan. The members from Bengal, Punjab, Sindh, NWFP, Baluchistan, and the sylnet district of Assam ceased to be the members of the constituent assembly for India, whereas West Bengal and East Punjab had fresh elections.

It may be added that when the constituent assembly convened on 31st October 1947 after partition the total membership stood at 299 out of which 70 were representatives of states. It however, redounds to the credit of the constituent assembly that all decision were taken by the voice vote and there was no division. Thus it may be said that the decisions were unanimous.

Subsequently, the draft constitution was introduced on 4th November 1948. The clause by consideration or second reading as it is called commenced on November 15 1948 and ended on 17th October 1949. It comprised several sessions. Eight major committees were constituted to deal with specific areas and a number of other minor committees were also constituted. It was the function of the drafting committee to give effect to the committees report and views in the draft constitution. The third reading began on 17th. November 1949 and was finished on 26th November 1949 on which date it was declared as passed.[36]

Again, some provisions resulting to citizenship, provisional parliament temporary and transitional provisions etc. came into effect on 26th November 1949. This is also the date mentioned in the preamble as the date on which the people of India adopted enacted and gave to themselves this constitution. The remaining provisions came into effect on 26th January 1950, which the constitution terms as the date of commencement.[37]

It is true that some scholars in this field were critical about the representative character of the Constituent Assembly. They argued that necessary arrangements were not made for convening a new Constituent Assembly on the basis of universal adult franchise. This demand, according to congress was not tenable on the ground that it would be too slow and cumbersome procedure and moreover it would also not be feasible in the existing Indian condition. The fact cannot be denied that congress made every effort to give the Assembly as broad-based a membership as possible. The representatives of various communities and their viewpoints were represented. Mention may be made in this context that due to liberal congress policy, minority communities were fully represented in the Constituent Assembly. As for example, the Indian Christians had seven representatives, the Anglo-Indian three, Parsis three and so on. After the partition, the minorities had 88 out of 235 seats allotted to the provinces in the assembly or 37 per cent of; the provincial membership. Not only that the ideological spectrum of the assembly was broadened by the inclusion of non-congress experts such as Dr. Radhakrishnan, N. Gopalswamy Ayyaanger etc. The Assembly also included such eminent women leaders like Sarojini Naidu and Hansa Mehta.As a matter of fact, the constituent Assembly had in it a galaxy of brilliant men including Dr. B.R. Ambedkar, Alladi Krishna Swamy Ayyar, Shivrao, H.N. Kunzru etc. who were non-Congress but had made their mark in different spheres of life.

It is important to note that because of the dominance of lawyers in the Assembly, and especially in the drafting committee, it was able to wield considerable power over the framing of the constitution. For instances, Dr. K.V. Rao has commented that Dr. Ambedkar treated the constituent Assembly like a tutorial class where students should be given a free choice to work and express their opinion while the teacher should have the last say. In fact, the dominance of lawyers in the drafting committee accounts for a certain legalistic character of the Indian Constitution.[38]

## References

1. Dutt R. Palme: India To-day reprint, June 1979.
2. Macaulaay: Speech in the House of Commons, July 1833.
3. *Ibid.*
4. Gladstone, letter to Sir James Graham, April 23 1858: "Life and letters of Sir James Graham", Vol. II, p. 340 quoted in R. Palme Dutta's: India To-day.
5. Lord Cromer: 'Ancient and Modern Imperialiasm', 1910 P12 quoted in R. Palme Dutt's India To-day, p. 486
6. Lord Moreley: Speech in the House of Lords, December 17 1908.
7. Viscount Morley: Speech in the House of Lords, February, 23, 1909 quoted in R. Pallme Dutt's India To-day p. 490.
8. *Ibid.*
9. Sharms B.K.: Introduction to the constitution of India New Delhi 2002 p. 5.
10. *Ibid.*
11. Quoted in Deshika Char, Readings in the Constitutional History of India, Oxford University Press, 1983 p. 487.
12. Basu, D.: Commentary on the Constitution of India Fourth edition, Calcutta, 1961 Vol. I p. 1.
13. Lloyd George, in the House of Commons on August 2,1922 Quoted by R.P. Dutt: India To-day, Calcutta. Reprint 1970 p. 500 India To-day, Calcutta, Reprint 1979 p. 500.
14. Winston Churchill: Speech to the Indian empire society December 11, 1930 quoted by R.P. Dutt: India To-day, p. 500.
15. Kapoor, A. C.: Select Constitutions, 1963 New Delhi p. 46.
16. Nehru, Jawaharlal: an autobiography, Oxfords University Press, New Delhi, Eighth impression, 1989 p. 574.
17. Kapoor, A. C. Ibid p. 47 quoted from the Indian constituent assembly p. 8.
18. *Ibid.*
19. *Ibid.*

20. Basu, D: Commentary on the constitution of India Vol. I p. 1-3.
21. Maulana Abul Kalam Azad: India Wins Freedom, 1988 p. 253-254.
22. Chandra Bipin etc.: Freedom struggle, National Book Trust, New Delhi p. 216.
23. *Ibid.*
24. *Ibid.*
25. Dutt, R. Palme: India To-day, Calcutta-1979 Reprint pp. 590-591.
26. Basu, D.: Ibid pp. 2-3.
27. *Ibid.*
28. *Ibid.*
29. *Ibid.*
30. Austin, Granville: Indian Constitution; Cornerstone of a Nation 1964.
31. Sharma B.K.: Introduction to the Constitution of India p. 23.
32. *Ibid.*
33. Sharma B.K.: Introduction to the Constitution of India p. 23.
34. *Ibid.*
35. *Ibid.*
36. *Ibid.*
37. *Ibid.*
38. *Ibid.*

# 3

# The Growth of Government

The growth of Parliamentary system in India is no recent invention. In fact, it has developed in a continuous line since the crown assumed all powers of the government from the East India Company. Queen Victoria's proclamation of November 1858 assured the Princes that all treaties and engagements with them would be honoured and scrupulously maintained.[1] The proclamation of 1858 was followed by the Indian Council act 1861 and later by the Indian council act 1892. Although the above Acts laid down the constitution and powers of the Governor in Council and the Governor General in council and that for the first time the British relaxed the rule that the council shall consist exclusively of officials. The Act permitted it to include additional members not less than six and not more than twelve nominated for two years. The Act also prescribed that not less than half of these would be non-official members. Such non-official people members were not elected representatives of the people but were handpicked by the government. The function of the council was restricted to making laws and regulations. No motion other than that relating to legislation could be introduced. Even for legislation predominant powers were vested in the Governor-General. For all-important bills his prior sanction was required. He could veto a bill or reverse it for assent of the crown. The Governor General could also legislate by ordinance.[2] Later the Indian councils act 1892 increased the number of additional members not less than 10 and not more than 16. The powers of the legislative councils were also increased. Rules framed under the act allowed the members to ask questions with subject to restrictions and to take part in the discussion on the budget.[3]

It is however worth noting that the pledges or promises to India of complete equality and disappearance of distinctions between rulers and ruled were not of course intended to be fulfilled in the broad sense in which they appeared to be made. Mention may be made in this context confidential letter written by Lord Lytton Viceroy (1876-80) to Lord Cranbrook, the secretary of state about the policy of British Government in India: "We all know that these claims and expectations never can or will be fulfilled. We had the choice between prohibiting straightforward course. This I am writing confidently, I do not hesitate to say that both the Government of England and of India appear to me up to the present moment unable to answer satisfactorily the charge of having taken every means in their power breaking to the heart the words of promise they have uttered to the ear".[4] Again Lord Salisbury in his downright fashion characterised the British pledges to India as 'political hypocrisy'. The real aim expressed in misleadingly flamboyant form in these pledges and proclamations of a bygone era, was the gradual extension of a carefully controlled subordinate association of Indians in the imperialist administrative machinery so as to have the support of a trained stratum of upper class and middle class Indians to assist in holding the masses in subjection.[5]

In 1861 the Indian councils act provided for the addition of six nominated non-official members to the viceroy's Legislative council; and some of these nominated members were carefully selected Indians. It is significant to note that like a new repressive weapon accompanied every subsequent reform measure, the 'reform' was accompanied by a new repressive weapon; the viceroy was given the power to issue ordinances having for six months at any time the force of law – a power freely used in the modern period.[6]

In 1883-84 the local self-government Acts introduced the elective principle into municipal government and established rural boards and district councils. Then in 1892 the Indian Councils Act added a few indirectly elected members who are actually recommended for approval not formally elected by the local government and other bodies to the provincial legislative councils, and through them at a further stage of indirectness to the viceroy's legislative council.[7]

The next landmark in the history of constitutional history in the Indian councils act of 1909 better known as the Morley-Minto reforms introduced an elected majority into the provincial legislative councils and an elected minority into the viceroy's legislative council. The functions of these councils remained severely restricted with no control over administration or finance. Their legislation could be vetoed if disappeared the franchise was extremely narrow and to the existing multiplication of electing bodies was added the system of separate Muslim electorates.

The Morley-Minto reforms were the first reforms to be carried in the midst of and as a result of widespread national agitation and demand for self-government and with the avowed political aim to defeat that agitation and in Morley's phrase 'rally the Moderates'. The reforms were first projected in 1906, following the great upswing of the national movement in 1905, the boycott and swadeshi campaign, which was launched in 1905, and the Russian revolution of 1905, which had shaken the other great oriental despotism of the Tsar. In this situation these minute reforms were presented with a great beating of the drums as the beginning of a new era.[8]

It is to be noted that Lord Morley's calculations to defeat the movement for self-government by his reforms were openly expressed. He thus analysed the situation: "....There are three classes of people whom we have to consider in dealing with a scheme of this kind. There are the extremists who nurse fantastic dreams that some day the will drive us out of India... The second group nourish no hopes of this sort, but hope autonomy or self-government of the colonial species and pattern. And then the third sections of this classification ask for no more than to be admitted to co-operation in our administration".[9] He also added, "I believe the effect of the reforms has been, is being and will be to draw the second class who hope for colonial autonomy, into the third class, who will be content with being admitted to a fair and full cooperation".[10]

Thus it is clear from the above statement that 'cooperation in our administration' along the path of constitutional reforms, was the chosen method of imperialism by which it hoped to defeat the national aim of self-government. There was no question at this time of presenting the reforms as "a step to self-government". Moreover, Lord Morley made it perfectly clear that the reforms were not to be regarded as leading "directly or indirectly to the establishment of a parliamentary system in India".

Lord Morley again emphasised the point, by writing to Lord

Minto that there was to be no question of any advance, then or in the future to responsible government in India. He remarked.[11] "Your Excellency's disclaimer for your government of being 'advocates of representative government for India in the western sense of the term is not more than was to be expected. Some of the most powerful advocates of the representative system in Europe have learned and taught from Indian experiences of their own that in your excellency's words, 'it could never be a kin to the instincts of the many races comprising the population of the Indian Empire' ... while repudiating the intension or desire to attempt the transplantation of any European form of representative government to Indian soil, what is sought by your excellency in council is to improve existing machinery, or to find new form for 'recognising the natural aspirations of educated men to share in the government of their country'. I need not to say that in this design you have the cordial concurrence of his majesty's government. He added, "One main standard and test for all who have a share in guiding Indian policy, whether at Whitehall or Calcutta, is the effect of whatever new proposal may at any time be made upon the strength and steadiness of the paramount power".[12]

So, the interests of the paramount power are decisive and the motive of the imperialistic power was to defeat the national aim of self-government.

The situation however changed during the war of 1914-18, the weakening of foundations of imperialism, the awakening of India, as of all the colonial peoples, Hindu-Muslim unity and the Congress-League scheme of 1916 for self-government and the Russian revolution of March 1917, opening the wave of popular advance in all countries and launching the slogans of national self-determination throughout the world.

In 1917, Lala Hardayal organised a revolutionary movement in the USA and Canada. Rash Behari Bose, Sachindra Nath Sanyal, Vishnu Ganesh Pingle, Baghi Kartar Singh and Bhai Paramanand planned an armed revolt. The 'D' day was 21 February 1915. It was detected because of the treachery of an individual. Raja Mahendra Pratap, V.N. Chattopadhyaya, Bhupen Dutta and Barkatulla tried to bring armed rebillion. Raja Mahendra Pratap set up a provisional government in Kabul. Bagha Jatin led the rebels in Bengal. V.D. Savarkar had already formed revolutionary groups in U.K. and Europe. Besides Chandrashekhar Azad, Ramprasad Bismil, Jogesh Chandra

Chatterjee, Bhagat Singh etc. formed the Hindusthan Republic Association, which took part in many terrorist activities, and most of them sacrificed their life for the cause of freedom.

Under such circumstances the First World War commenced. The British needed India's cooperation in terms of man and money. This forced them to declare a change in the imperialistic policy. The congress party was under the control of radicals. Smt. Annie Besant and others had launched 'Home Rule Movement' and in response to the popular demand His Majesty's Government made an announcement on 20th August 1917, E.S. Montagu, secretary of state for India made it before the House of Commons. The statement was: "The policy of his majesty's government, with which the government of India are in complete accord, is that of increasing association of Indians in every branch of the administration and the gradual development of self governing institutions with a view to progressive realisation of responsible government in India as an integral part of the British Empire".[13]

Now with a view to prepare a scheme of reforms Montagu came to India in 1917. Immediately coming over here he met the Indian leaders and tried to understand their grievances and aspirations. In consultation with the Governor-General Lord Chemsford he prepared "The Report on constitutional Reforms which came to be known as 'Montford Report' was published in July 1918 and became the base for the Government of India act, 1919. The governing principles of the 'Montford' were in the shape of four formulae:[14]

1. There should be, as far as possible, complete popular control in local bodies and the largest possible independence for them of outside control.

2. The provinces are the domains in which the earlier steps towards the progressive realization of responsible government should be taken. Some measure of responsibility should be given at once, and our aim is to give complete responsibility as soon as conditions permit. This involves at once giving the provinces the largest measure of independence, legislative, administrative and financial, of the Government of India, which is compatible with the due discharge by the latter of its own responsibilities.

3. The Government of India must remain wholly responsible to parliament, and saving such responsibility; its authority in essential

matters must remain indisputable, pending experience of the effect of the changes now to be introduced in the provinces. In the meantime the Indian Legislative council should be enlarged and made more representative and its opportunities of influencing Government increased.

4. In proportion as the foregoing changes take effect, the control of Parliament and the Secretary of state over the Government of India and provincial Governments must be relaxed.

Mention may be made in this context that the Indian Statutory commission, popularly known as the Simon commission has, however rightly observed that the above governing principles struck at the three essential features of the system of Government obtaining in India hither to, viz., (a) the concentration of authority at the centre, (b) the control over legislative functions exercised by the Executive, and (c) the ultimate responsibility of parliament for the whole of Indian Government.[15]

It is important to note that the publication of the Joint Report on Indian constitutional Reforms which had chiefly enunciated certain general principles of reform, was followed by the Government of India Bill which was introduced into the House of Commons in 1919 by Mr. Montague, Secretary of State for India, The Bill as it emerged from the Joint Select Committee, became on 23rd December, 1919 the Government of India Act, 1919. This Act is popularly known as the Reforms of 1919 or the Montague Chelmsford Reforms which provided not only for the classification of functions of Government as central and Provincial, but also, unlike the Reforms of 1909, for the partial introduction of the parliamentary system of government into the provincial field in the major provinces of British India, distinguished as Governors' Provinces. Thus, the provinces were divided between those which were made over to popular control and those which for the time being remained in official hands. The former were called the transferred subjects and the latter the Reserved subjects.[16]

As a result, each Governor's Province was governed, in relation to the reserved subjects, by a Governor in Council and in relation to the Transferred subjects, ordinarily, by the Governor acting with ministers appointed from among the elected members of the provincial Legislative council. The guiding principles to include in the transferred list those department which afford most opportunity for local knowledge and social service, those in which Indians have shown themselves to be keenly interested and those which stand most in need of development. However, for the administration of the transferred subjects the Governor of a province was empowered by law to appoint ministers and the latter held office during his pleasure. In fact the power of the Governor to choose his ministers was limited because the ministers are supposed to be the elected members of the legislative council. Naturally, it was not possible for a minister who did not enjoy the confidence of the council to remain long in office. Thus, ministers were responsible to the provincial Legislative Council in the Parliamentary sense. The Parliamentary Joint Committee however observes: Ministers who enjoy the confidence of a majority in their legislative council the fullest opportunity of managing that field of Government which is entrusted to their care. In their work they will be assisted and guided by the Governor, who will accept their advice and promote their policy whenever possible if he finds himself compelled to act against their advice, it will only be in circumstances roughly analogous to those in which he has to override his executive council – circumstances which will be indicated in the Instrument of Instructions furnished to him on his appointment by his Majesty.[17] Thus, although in limited sense, the Act of 1919 introduced the responsible government in the provinces but at the centre no element of responsible government was introduced. The Governor General-in-council continued to be responsible as before to the British Parliament only.

In response to the growing political discontent in India, the Government of India Act of 1935 came into being. This phase, in a general way, was only a further extension of the principle of responsible government. It is true that the Government of India Act, 1935 provided not only for the abolition of diarchy from the provincial sphere and the introduction of practically full responsible Government there but also for the introduction of what we may conveniently characterize as diarchy into the sphere of the Government of India.[18] It implies that, so far as the Centre was concerned, there was to be for the administration of what we may call the transferred Departments, a Council of Ministers, not exceeding ten in number to aid and advise the Governor General in the exercise of his functions, except in so far as he was by or under the Act of 1935, required to exercise his functions or any of them at his discretion.

It is interesting to note that the Governor General was empowered by the said Act to exercise his "individual judgement" in certain cases and in this aspect his ministers would have a constitutional right to tender advice to him, but this advice was not to be binding on him and he could act, notwithstanding such advice, in such a manner as he would deem requisite for the discharge of his responsibilities. Moreover, in respect of both these sets of matters, the Governor General was empowered to take action notwithstanding an adverse vote of the central legislature whether such a vote related to the passage of legislation or to the appropriation of funds.[19]

As regards administration of Reserved Departments, the Governor-General was empowered to appoint at his discretion not more than three counsellors and whereas, the council of Ministers at the centre was to be responsible to the central legislature, the responsibility of the Governor-General in respect of matters in which he was empowered to act in his discretion or to exercise his individual judgment was to be to the secretary of state for India.[20] It is thus evident that the Government of India Act of 1935 contemplated a federation congesting of British Indian provinces and native states. Legislative powers of the centre and the component units were demarcated through three lists. Viz., the central list, Provincial list and the concurrent list. The constituency pattern, however, based upon communal and other sectarian interests remained more or less unaltered.

It is interesting to note that although the key to the constitution of 1935 was the conception of Federation, professor A.B. Keith, the leading constitutional authority in Britain did not fail to comment, "it is difficult to resist the impression that either responsible government should have been frankly declared impossible or the reality conceded. It is not surprising that neither gratitude nor co-operation is readily forthcoming for a hybrid product such as is the system of special responsibilities and acts to be done according to individual judgment".[21] He also adds, "for the federal scheme it is difficult to feel any satisfaction. The units of which it is composed are too disparate to be joined suitably together, and it is too obvious that on the British side the Scheme is favoured in order to provide an element of pure conservatism in order to combat any dangerous elements of democracy contributed by British India".[22]

Now, with the changes in the international political scene and more particularly the conditions in India and Britain led the British government to an unequivocal acceptance of Indians claim to freedom. On and from the 15th of August, 1947, full and unqualified responsible government was established at the centre and in the Provinces of the Dominion of India under the Government of India act 1935, as adopted by the Governor General of India in the exercise of the powers conferred on him by the Indian Independence Act, 1947 and the Governor-General as well as the Governor of provinces became purely constitutional Heads of their respective Governments. This state of affairs continued till the inauguration of the Republic of India on 26th January 1950 as envisaged by the constitution of India adopted on 26th November 1949 by the Constituent Assembly of India. Thus, the new constitution after several parleys between Indian leaders and Britain finally provided for the establishment of the parliamentary system of government both at the centre and in the constituent states of the Indian union.

Indian people might have felt proud that they have weathered many storms and have lived to witness the liquidation-voluntary or compulsory whatever might be, of the biggest empire of the world over which the sun never sets. Their cherished goal, viz. the attainment of independence is no longer a dream but an accomplished fact and it rests entirely on their sweet will either to remain as an integral part of British Empire or to sever that feeble link, the remnant of their political slavery. But although the British have left us free to mould the future in our own way, we cannot possibly rid ourselves so soon of the institutions built, so assiduously by the foreign rulers in our country. It goes without saying that the existing system of law, education and administration is the direct outcome of British rule in India. Chakraborty (1968) observes: "while not being blind to the denationalising influences of the British rule in this country, we must also be alive to the gains we have reaped by coming into contact with a people who have; made definite contributions to the progress of civilisation". The new constitution of India bears unmistakable stamp of its indebtedness to the Government of India Act, 1935 in so far as the size, contents and inclusion of miscellaneous matters are concerned.

Probably, the greatest achievement of the new constitution is the integration and democratisation of those of the former Native

States and chief commissioners' Provinces that remained in India after partition where as the Government of India act, 1935 simply ignored the rights of these people to their legitimate emancipation.

However, a historical survey of our constitutional development bears testimony to the fact that like any other constitution, Indian constitution is based on social, political and economic relevancy which constituted the philosophy of its own .In this context, the content of the 'objectives Resolution' moved by Pandit Nehru and adopted by the constituent Assembly on 22nd January, 1947 will not be irrelevant. The contents of the objectives resolutions were:[23]

1. This constituent Assembly declares its final and firm resolve to proclaim India as an Independent Sovereign Republic and to draw up for her future governance a constitution;

2. Wherein the territories that now comprise British India the territories that now form the India States, and such other parts of India, as are outside British India and the states as well as such other territories as are willing to be constituted into the Independent Sovereign India, shall be a Union of them all;

3. Where in the said territories whether with their present boundaries or with such others as may be determined by the constituent Assembly and thereafter according to the law of the constitution, shall possess and retain the status of autonomous units, together with residuary powers and exercise all powers and functions of government and administration, save and except such powers and functions as are vested in or assigned to the union or as are inherent or implied in the Union or resulting there from;

4. Where in all power and authority of the Sovereign Independent India, its constituent parts and organs of Government are derived form the people;

5. Wherein shall be guaranteed and secured to all people of India justice – social, economic and political, equality of status, of opportunity and before the law, freedom of thought, expression, belief, faith, worship, vocation, association and action, subject to law and public morality;

6. Wherein adequate safeguards shall be provided for minorities, backward and tribal areas, and depressed and other backward classes;

7. Wherein shall be maintained the integrity of the territory of the Republic and its sovereign rights on land, sea and air according to justice and the law of civilised nations and

8. This ancient land attain its rightful and honoured place in the world and make its full and willing contribution to the promotion of world peace and the welfare of mankind.

From the aforesaid 'objective Resolutions' moved by Pandit Nehru, it became clear that the influence of socialist ideas within the national movement and the popularising of relation of socialism to nationalism found typical expression. He brought to the forefront the close connection between national liberation and social liberation. It is quite relevant to point out that in his presidential address to the Lucknow national congress in 1936, Jawharlal Nehru emphatically stated: "I work for Indian independence because the nationalist in me cannot tolerate alien domination; I work for it even more because for me it is the inevitable step to social and economic change. I should like the congress to become a socialist organisation and to join hands with the other forces in the world that are working for the new civilisation. But I realise that the majority of the congress, as it is constituted to-day, may not be prepared to go thus far ... Much as I wish for the advancement of socialism in this country, I have no desire to force the issue on the congress and thereby create difficulties in the way of our struggle for independence. I shall cooperate gladly and with all the strength in me with all those who work for independence, even though they do not agree witr the socialist solution. But I shall do so stating my position frankly and hoping in course of time to convert the congress and the country to it, for only thus can I see it achieving independence".[15]

Hence, there is no doubt, and it is becoming increasingly clear to progressive Indian opinion, that the final solution of Indian problems can only be achieved along socialist lines. Only socialist industry and collective agriculture can finally provide the means which will raise India from a world slum to a land of plenty and happiness.[16]

The above ideal embodied in the objectives Resolution is truly reflected in the preamble to the constitution for which K.M. Munshi, a member of the Drafting committee of the constituent Assembly proudly describe it as 'Political horoscope'.

## References

1. Sharma, B.K.: Introduction to the constitution of India, New Delhi, 2002 p. 1.
2. *Ibid.*
3. *Ibid.*
4. Dutt, R. Palme: India To-day p. 488.
5. *Ibid.*
6. *Ibid.*
7. *Ibid.*
8. *Ibid.*
9. *Ibid.*
10. Viscount Morley, Speech in the House of Lords, February 23, 1909 quoted in R. Palme Dutt's India To-day.
11. Lord Morley to Lord Minto, quoted in the Montage Chelmsford Report p. 64.
12. *Ibid.*
13. Debates on Indian Affairs: House of Lords (1909) quoted in Desika Char: Readings in Constitutional History of India, 1983 p. 457.
14. Banerjee D. N.: Some aspects of the Constitution of India pp. 3-4.
15. Report of the Indian Statutory Commission Vol. !, 1930, para 139 and also para 127.
16. Report of the Parliamentary joint Select Committee on the Government of India Bill, 1919 para 5.
17. *Ibid.*
18. *Ibid.*
19. *Ibid.*
20. Banerjee, D. N.: Some aspects of the Constitution of India p. 11.
21. Keith, A. B.: A Constitutional History of India 1600-1935 pp. 473-474.
22. *Ibid.*
23. *Ibid.*
24. Jawharlal Nehru: Presidential address to the Lucknow National Congress, 1936.
25. Dutt., R.P.: India To-day p. 638.

# 4

# Crisis in Indian Politics

The constitution of India declares, "India, that is Bharat, shall be a union of states". The word 'union' of course, does not indicate any particular type of federation as it is used also in the preamble of the constitution of United States, which is known as the model of federation. In the preamble of the British North America act which according to Lord Haldane, did not create a true federation at all.[1] Again, in the preamble to the Union of South Africa act 1909, which patently set up a unitary constitution, and even in the constitution of USSR (1977), which formally acknowledges a right of secession (Art. 72) to each republic, that is unit of union.[2] It is to be noted in this context that while submitting the draft constitution, Dr. Ambedkar, the chairman of Drafting committee, stated that "although its constitution may be federal in structure", the committee had used the term "union" because of certain advantages.[3]

These advantages according to Dr. Ambedkar were to indicate two things, viz., (a) that the Indian federation is not the result of an agreement by the units and (b) the component units have no freedom to secede from it.[4]

Now let us examine whether the essence of federalism got incorporated in our constitution. Mention may be made that a six-judge bench of the Supreme Court went into the matter in detail in 'state of West Bengal' v union of India.[5] The Coal Bearing Areas, which vested in the state of West Bengal, were acquired by Coal Bearing Areas (acquisition and development) Act 1957, states case before the Supreme Court was this act totally destroyed the federal principle and was therefore, 'ultra vires'. This required the bench to examine the form of federation adopted by our constitution because one of the principal arguments advanced by the state was that the constitution having adopted the federal principle of government the state shares the sovereignty of the nation with the union and therefore power of parliament does not extend to enacting legislation for depriving the states of property vested in them as sovereign authorities. Entrustment of power to legislate must therefore be so read as to imply a restriction upon the parliament's power under entry 42 of list III when it is sought to be exercised in respect of the property owned by a state[6]. In this context B.P Sinha, the learned Chief Justice stated that ever since the assumption of authority by the British crown under statue 21 and 22 vict (1858) ch 106, the administration of British India was unitary and highly centralised. The Governor General was invested with autocratic powers to administer the entire territory. Even though the territory was divided into administrative units the authority of the respective governors of the provinces was derived from the Governor General and he was responsible to the British parliament. Some process of devolution took place under government of India act 1919 but that was only for the purpose of decentralisation of the governmental power but on that account government did not cease to be unitary. The aim of the Government of India act 1935 was to unite the provinces and Indian states into a federation but that could be achieved only if a substantial number of the Indian states agreed to join the provinces in the federation. For diverse reasons the Indian states never joined the proposed federation and the part dealing with federation never became active. In the provinces, however, certain alteration were made certain departments were administered with the aid of Ministers, who were popularly elected and who were in essence responsible to the electorate. The Governor was still authorised to act in his discretion without consulting his ministers in respect of certain matters. He derived his authority from the British crown and was subject to the directions which the central government gave relating to execution of the acts of the central legislature and for the maintenance of means of communication and for preventing grave menace to peace or tranquillity. Thus, the administration continued to function as an agent of the British parliament[7].

In the next phase by the Indian Independence act 1947, a separate dominion of India was carved out and by section 6 thereof the legislature was for the first time authorised to make laws for the dominion. The British parliament since then ceased to function and to that extent the Indian dominion became sovereign. Subsequently in 1950 the new constitution came into force. No doubt the territory was too big for a democratic set up with wholly centralised form of government. Imposition of centralised form might have also meant a reversal of political trend, which had led to the decentralisation of administration and distribution of power. Hansaria (1998) observed: "The constitution had therefore to be in a form in which authority was decentralised. In the era immediately prior to the enactment of Indian independence act, there were partially autonomous units such as the provinces. There were Indian states, which were in essence sovereign, but their sovereignty was extinguished by the various merger agreements, which the rulers of those states entered into with government of India before the constitution. By virtue of the process of integration of the various states there emerged a centralised form of administration in which the Governor General was the fountainhead of executive authority".[8]

It is thus clear that India had a thoroughly unitary constitution under the government of India Acts 1935. The provincial governments were virtually the agents of the central government, deriving powers by the delegation from the latter. To appreciate the mode of formation of federation in India, we must go back to the government of India Act 1935, which for the first time introduced the federal concept in the constitution act. And by the same Act of 1935, the British Parliament set up a federal system in the same manner as it had done in the case of Canada, viz. by creating autonomous units and combining them into a federation by one and the same Act.[9] It did not emerge out of any federal sentiment, nor did it come into being as a result of compact or agreement between existing states to delegate some of their powers to a common government. All powers hither to exercised in India were resumed by the crown and redistributed between the federation and the provinces by a direct grant. Under this system, the provinces derived their authority directly from the crown and exercised legislative and executive powers, broadly free from central control within a defined sphere. Nevertheless, the centre retained control through the governor's 'special responsibilities' and his obligation to exercise his individual judgement and discretion in certain matters and the power of the centre to give directions to the provinces.[10]

As a matter of fact, the founding fathers were under no obligation to accept the form of government or federation as reflected in the 1935 act. Yet they deliberately converted a unitary system into a federal one. Scholars in the field of constitutional history belive that the colonial experiences threw up forces which were to provide both the basis and the limits of India's federal experiment at the outset. Once the national movement reached the mass mobilisation phase, it had to come to grips with a pluralistic social base with stable ethno-linguistic territorial identities, many with ancient historical roots. The congress recognised fairly early the enormous socio-political force potential of these identities in giving the freedom struggle a broader base. It sought to evolve an organisational framework for their integration and political mobilisation: the pradesh emerged almost naturally and had no difficulty in being recognised as the basic territorial unit.[11]

They also added that federalism as an institutional device was proposed by the colonial power in a calculatedly different perspective as a part of its strategy, to contain the growing popularity of the national movement. It sought to gain acceptability for a power sharing arrangement, which would ensure communal representation: these forces were impelled by the separate electorates to undertake a parallel mobilisation process on the basis of crosscutting religious cleavages. Further, the princely state's arguments in favour of considerable autonomy were readily accepted by the colonial power: this was calculared to dampen antifeudal and nationalistic ardour of their peoples to curb the spread of national liberation movement.[12] Moreover, the strong centre ideology was premised on the lack of confidence in institutions embedded in the local context. They were variously considered incompetent irresponsible, insufficient and unreliable.[13]

Hence, the federal structure conceived in the Indian Constitution embodies strong elements of unitary form of governments having sweeping powers out of a fear that if state governments are given more powers, disintegrating tendencies may lead to the break up of the foundation of the federation. The founding fathers in fact, built a constitutional structure with a powerful central government envisaging the emergence of an indivisible and integrated India, As a matter of fact, India has got to put up with this in view of the past history of the country and danger of centrifugal forces still operating in it in the shape of regionalism, linguilism, fundamentalism and other anti-national tendencies. But in reality, the fact also remains that despite the country having a strong central government, it is still facing serious challenges of regionalism, secessionism, etc. This trend has made many politicians as well as political scientists raise questions about the appropriateness of; the federal structure laid down in the constitution of India.

From the internal dynamics of the socio-politico background of the Indian constitution with the Westminster model of government with its 86 amendments in forty-six years, whereas in America, during the same length of time the constitution was amended for ten times only. In fact, the process of formal amendment prescribed by the American constitution to changes in Social conditions has fallen into the hands of the judiciary even though it ostensibly exercises the function only of interpreting the constitution. Instead of leaving the matter to the slow machinery of judicial interpretation our constitution has vested the power in the people's representatives and, though the final power of interpretation of the constitution as it stands at any moment belongs to the courts, the power of changing the instrument itself has been given to parliament (with or without ratification by the state legislatures) and, if parliament, acting as the constituent body, considers that the interests of the country so require, it can amend the Constitution as often as it likes. The case with which the amendments have been enacted demonstrates that our constitution contains the potentiality of peacefully adopting changes some of, which would be considered as revolutionary in other countries.[14]

Basu (1998) observes: "The real question involved in this context is whether it is the judiciary or a constituent body which should be entrusted with the task of introducing changes in order to keep pace with the exigencies of national and social progress. For reasons good or bad, the framers of our constitution preferred the legislature as the machinery for introducing changes into the constitution, but the need for change is acknowledged even in countries like the USA where the task has been assumed by the judiciary, taking advantage of the fact that the amending machinery provided in the constitution was too heavy and unwieldy for practical purposes".[15] A little reflection will show that some of these changes, the need for which must be admitted even by critics, could not have been introduced by the courts, by the application of the canons of statutory interpretation which are firmly embedded in our courts. An instance to the point is the insertion of the word 'reasonable' to quality the word 'restrictions' in cl. (2) of Art.19 (by the first amendment). Without such a qualification, the engine of judicial review would have been altogether excluded from the field of legislative encroachment upon the freedom of expression, for, it was not open to any court, unless it was determined to do violence to the canons of interpretation, to supply the word 'reasonable' which had been inserted by the makers of the constitutions in all other clauses of the article but omitted from cl. (2) of Art.19. It may be stated in this context that the 42nd Amendment Act of 1976, by which Congress Government, taking advantage of its monolithic control over the union as well as the State Legislatures, effected comprehensive changes in the Constitution, overturning some of its bed rocks.[16] Basu adds, "so widespread and drastic was the impact of this amendment that it would be proper to call it an Act for 'revision' rather than 'amendment' of the constitution". Subsequently however, due to popular resentment against such drastic changes, the Janata party was voted to power at the general elections which was held as a result of dissolution of the Lok Sabha at the instance of Mrs. Gandhi early in 1977 and the Janata government was succeeded in enacting the 43rd and 44th amendment Acts (1977, 1978) wiping out many of the new provisions introduced by the 42nd Amendment Act, restored in the Pre-1976 text of the constitution on many points.

There is no doubt, that with the Westminster model as adopted by the framers of the Indian constitution both at the Union and state, the British cabinet system is a complicated outcome of history and the sagacity of trained politicians and even then, some scholars believe that, it is a difficult task to formulate clear-cut propositions relating to the conventions upon which the system is founded. Survey record shows that average life of a chief Minister since the later half of the eighties is fifteen months only. Legislators look upon their tenure as a financial investment. They constantly interfere with the functioning of the administration at all levels. Almost in the same tune in the centre, no sooner does a Prime Minister come to power then the dissidents get busy trying to pull him down. Naturally, he has to make compromises not only to gain power but also to retain power. Even while the party is in power, there is a frequent change in the head of the government. All this has not only promoted instability and corruption but also brought administration to a halt resulting in lack of proper checks and balances, the government has ceased to be either a fair umpire or a good ruler and its oppressive economic burden with bloated bureaucracies including public sector and over sized cabinets and political plunder through wide-spread political patronage has brought the economy to a state of acute crisis.[17]

Fifty years' experience of the working of the constitution since 1947 shows that the system of parliamentary democracy is not workable in Indian conditions. If we analyse the political evolution of the party system in India we shall find five phases of growth, which will rather conclusively prove that Westminster model of government is hardly compatible. The phases are:

*The First Phase (1947-1968)*: This phase is envisaged as a one party dominant system. During this period, that is, from 1947-1967 Indian National Congress was the extra-powerful political party. Moreover, the charismatic leadership of the National congress especially of Nehru and Sardar Patel gave the Indian National Congress Party a position of unique political dominance over the other smaller political parties having little or no opposition from them. It is interesting to note that the Indian National Congress was founded mainly through the efforts and initiative of a British civil Servant, Allan Ocavian Hume by name. For a long time the Congress remained extremely loyal to the British Government. It only became nationalist after the First World War, when Mahatma Gandhi became the defecto leader of the Congress. Again, it would be a profound error to regard the Congress merely as a political party. In fact, it was an organised expression of the hopes and aspirations of the Indian people, the rallying centre of all progressive forces in the vast sub-continent. The congress included Muslims, Sikhs, Hindus, and big businessmen, industrialists side by side with poor peasants from the remote corners of the country. It claimed among its follower's agitators from the native states, Anglo-Indians Native Christians, Socialists and even reactionaries as well. The fact remains that almost all other small parties in India are the off-shoots of the Indian National Congress. Mention may be made that a good number of leaders of various political parties, viz., Communist party of India, Communist Party of India (Marxist), Forward Bloc, Muslim League, Hindu Mahasabha were associated with the National Congress Party. As a result, the successful working of the English presupposes the existence of two great parties each strong enough to restrain the violence of the other was remarkably absent in Indian political culture. Practically speaking, the peculiar giant size of the congress in proportion to the Lilliputian size of the opposition parties helped the former to bend parliamentary institutions to its own needs. In support of this statement reference may be made that in 1955 Prime Minister Nehru did not care to maintain the chastity of parliamentary practice. He decided to declare Bombay as a city of special status even without cabinet decision and in protest C.D. Deshmukh resigned from central Ministry.[18] Ghose (1991) aptly remarked: "It is unfortunate that Nehru never used his position and influence in the public life to resist the pressures of the economic strata in which he was born and above which he was genuinely inclined to rise at least in spirit and pragmatic thought".[19]

As a matter of fact, Nehru's economic policy of deficit financing for the period from 1956-61 was directly responsible for big inflation, massive unemployment, and untold hardship for the masses. His policy was also responsible for the rise in corruption and crimes. Such decision was taken of course, not to stir the hornet's nest as the ruling party received big donations from the grain lobby that had been granted the entire food production-cum pricing monopoly. The donations kept pouring in, aided by deficit financing, a recurring feature of most subsequent Five year plans. The operative point is that Nehru's social strata made him a big use of the Westminster system.

The above analysis of the working of the constitution during its first phase from 1947 to 1967 reveals that the Indian National Congress Party under the leadership of Nehru continued to be the strongest and the biggest political party in India and had shown a tendency to bend parliamentary institution to its needs.

*The Second Phase (1967-1975)* : This phase is characterised as the period of instability and uneasy transition to a multi-party situation. In fact, the years following the death of Nehru (1964) were marked by narrow struggle for power within the Congress party. It is also important to note that Nehru's Charismatic leadership helped him to resist the coherence of regional parity by offering concessions to regionalist sentiments within the party and also sporadic movements from outside like linguistic reorganisation of the states on the one hand and official language policy on the other. In these cases, congress however functioned as a federation of regionalist units. But after the death of Nehru, Lal Bahadur Shastri's vacillation over the 'Hindi' issue saw the emergence of Dravida Munnetra

Kazhagam (DMK) in Tamil Nadu as the first major regionalist force to capture power. In its programmes, the DMK identified. Tamilian poverty due to lack of industrialisation and for this the northerners alone were held to be responsible and this trend as a result led to anti-Hindi feeling. Subsequently, however, the DMK showed pragmatism when it allied with the national parties for electoral gains.

Parallel with the parties on national basis, a large number of parties have been organised on regional basis during this second phase. The activities of these regional parties are confined to a particular state or region. Regional sentiments and demands were also articulated by a number of breakaway congress groups such as Vishal Haryana or the Jana Congress in various States and the Akali Dal's emergence as the most powerful advocate of Punjabi linguistic community. As a result of new trend of regional political parties, the 1967 election had created a situation in which the Congress dominance was strikingly reduced. Congress lost power for the first time after the period of long thirty years in six states. This brought a number of opposition parties to the forefront, which again intensified inter-party conflict. These new developments according to congress are threats to the survival of India as a nation. The centralist argument of congress became more hardened after the split of congress in 1969 into two divisions, viz., Congress (I) and Congress (O). The Congress (I) controlled by Indira Gandhi followed a broad-based strategy keeping an eye open to the ensuing general election such as nationalisation of banks, abolition of privy purses and 'Garibi Hotao'. It is interesting to note that in spite of strong opposition Congress (I) won a thumping majority capturing 350 out of 520 seats.[20] But the strategy did not bring the desired fruit. Specially, national economy was marked by deep inflation, acute food shortages along with massive unemployment. Economic crisis was followed by political agitations like the 'Nava Nirman' in Gujrat in 1973, the all India Railway strike in 1974 and the climax being Allahabad High courts judgement debarring Indira Gandhi from contesting election for a long period of six years causing destabilisation in India gravely. Indira Gandhi immediately appealed to the Supreme Court by unanimous decision of her party. A big controversy and the stepping up of Jay Prakash Narayan's civil Disobedience Movement followed this. This political movement was considered as law and order problem of the country to be dealt with firmly and finally emergency was declared in June 1975 wherein many excesses had been committed and many had suffered. It is, however, curious to note that the J. P. Movement and the Allahabad High court judgement on the election petition case filed against Indira Gandhi by Raj Navain peaked around the same time. Some scholars are of opinion that in the interest of India's stability, the Judge could and should have confined himself to setting aside Indira Gandhi's election at the previous parliament polls instead of debarring her for the long period of six years.[21]

*The Third phase (1975-1977)* : This phase is marked by the emergency regime of Indira Gandhi ensuring credibility of the government in a context as emotive as it was stiffed when opinions had polarised and when the desired effect of a fall in essential prices was already discernible within a fortnight of the promulgation but at the some time it accelerated the process of institutional decline and the weakening of the parliamentary system by suspending civil liberties particularly freedom of the press and representative government. Judicial review of Maintenance of Internal Security Act (MISA) was suspended under the emergency. In any event MISA arrests and detentions were always kept confidential by the administration. The Government came down heavily on News papers, Press censorship was decided upon and every daily published in state capitals sent through a evening every representative, usually a senior man to the state Government's information wing for consideration wherein total materials were drastically censored under government seal? No criticism of the government was allowed or tolerated. Any attack on the Prime Minister's authority was considered to be an attack on the party as well on the nation's unity. Important decisions like the declaration of the emergency in 1975 and subsequently the postponement of the general election in 1976 and even the decision to general election in 1977 were not consulted in the cabinet meeting.[22] As a matter of fact, extra-constitutional centres of power and authority came into existence under the cover of emergency. She not only forfeited the credibility and trust of most, including the fawning Congressmen, she destroyed the moral fabric of the administration. The people became the fount of corruption and the source of extra-constitutional power.[23] Reference may be made about the Nagarwala case in which in the name of 'Mataji' Nagarwala could withdraw lakhs of money from the state Bank on a telephone call, was just one of the example only. It failed to see the judicial light of day and Nagarwala never lived to tell the truth.[24]

*The fourth phase (1977-1990)* : The emergency period from 1975 to 1977, was, in fact, one person show, no regional leadership, no cadres, no democracy, only the one-up-man ship of false populist politics without grassroots programmes. The advisers of Indira Gandhi were deteriorated into minions scheming to further her whims. She planted on court, party and government that extra-constitutional authority. Sanjoy son of Indira Gandhi whose Tughlak–like ways complemented her's and led to emergency and defeat in the 1977 elections.[25]

It is interesting to note that in the post-emergency 1977 election, almost all the non-congress (I) parties joined together in the form of Janata Party to confront the Congress through the merger of the Bharatiya Jana Sangh, the Socialist Party, the Bharatiya Lok Dal and the Congress (O). After the election, the Congress for Democracy (CFD), a breakaway group from the Congress led by Jagjivan Ram also joined the Janata Party. The Akali Dal and the CPI (M) effected seat adjustment with the Janata Party resulting in the defeat of the Congress. As a result, Janata won 43 per cent of the popular vote and 55 percent of the seats. And this was for the first time; a non-congress government at the centre governed India. The result was also spectacular in the state Assembly elections held in June 1977 and February 1978. The Janata Party gained control of nine of the seventeen state governments. The electorate outcome of 1977 was more a protest against the emergency regime of congress than keeping confidence on Janata party's leadership. As a matter of fact, the heterogeneous composition of the Janata Party and the strong ambitions of its leaders often in conflict with each other shattered the aspirations on the question of the stability of the government even for the scheduled period. It is true that in 1977 the Congress was defeated and Janata Party with the blessings of Jaya Prakash Narayan formed a government with Morarji Desai as Prime Minister whose coalition government was bound to end sooner or later. The Morarji Desai Government's exit was engineered by the charan Singh's lieuteuant, Raj Narain, a cabinet Minister in both Morarji and immediately succeeding Charan Singh Governments. The Morarji Government held office for more than two years while the Charan Singh Government functioned for less than six months before being brought down by Raj Narains defection – Cum-destabilisation and somersault.[26]

The divergent ideologies and political aspirations of the leaders put a heavy strain on the Janata experiment leading to its ultimate failure. Within a short time the party was disintegrated in mid 1979. Of course, the congress also did not remain intact. It split for the second time in 1978. The Congress led by Indira Gandhi, that is congress (I) appeared to be the only coherent party. This image helped Congress (I) to take advantage of the disunity in the Janata and as a result, in 1979's General Election Indira Gandhi again came to power with an impressive two third majority of the Lok-Sabha but centre state relation specially between Delhi and Punjab was not favourable the reason being that since the presentation by the Akali Dal around 1976 of basically economic demands, the centre took on inordinately long time in settling the demands passed by the *Anandpur Sahib* Resolution. Mention may be made about the *Anandpur Sahib* resolution placing the basic demands like a higher share of the Bhakranangal Dam waters, a better remunerative price for the wheat with which Punjab feeds almost the rest of India and Chandigarh as Capital for Punjab.[27] Out of these three basic demands Indira Gandhi granted the last one that is chandigarh as capital for Punjab and accordingly a date was set by her for the transferor Chandigarh to the Government of Punjab by Januuary / February 1984 at the latest. But the decision was apposed by Bhajn Lal, the then Chief Minister of Haryana on the plea that time was inadequate for the Haryana Government, then using Chandigarh an its capital. Subsequently however, Bhajan Lal had agreed in principle to the setting up of its new capital in Panipat. On the day before the formal handing over of Chandigarh by Dr. Alexender, there were big riots in panipat allegedly inspired by Bhajanlal's associates and as a result, the formal transfer of Chandigarh was postponed. Relation gravely deteriorated between Delhi and Bhindranwale's militants. The worsening of relation led to operation Blue star at Amritsar Golden Temple by the Indian army and this sort of action, in the opinion of political observer, led to Indira Gandhi's is assassination on October 31, 1984.

In the Political horizon of India a new political situation emerged after the assassination of Mrs. Gandhi. A wave of unparallel emotional support led the Congress (I) Party under the leadership of Rajib Gandhi to a historic victory in the General Election of 1985. The Congress (I) and its allies secured 415 Look-Sabha seats setting an all-time record. The political situation, however, did not remain intact in the next General Election of 1989 when polarisation was inevitable between the Congress (I) in alliance with AIADMK in Tamil Nadu and National Conference in JK States on the one side and the National Front Constituting Janata Dal, Telegu Desam, DMK. Assam Ganaparishad and Congress(S) on the other. The election yielded a divided verdict with the Congress (I) 184 seats whereas the National Front 145, the BJP 82 and the left Front 55 seats only.[28] President R. Venkataraman invited Rajiv Gandhi, the leader of the single largest party to form government but he declined. The president then invited Mr. V.P. Singh of National Front to form a government. The President of Course, received declaration of support to the National Front from the BJP and the left Front on 23rd October 1990. But as the BJP withdrew its support from the National Front, circumstances forced V.P. Singh to face trust vote on November 7, 1990. Mr. Singh complained that certain businessmen from Calcutta and Bombay were camping in Delhi to influence the members of Parliament to vote against him in the trust vote. He failed to secure trust vote and as a result V.P. Singh's government lasted for approximately one-year only.[29]

It is, thus obvious that the majority of India's voters rejected the Congress (I), which however managed to continue to poll the highest vote and win the highest number of seats as a single political party.

*The Fifth Phase (1990 till present day)* : On November 9, 1990 the President invited Congress (I) once again to form a government but instead of accepting the invitation, Rajiv Gandhi offered unconditional support to Chandrasekhar. The President then invited BJP and the Left Front serially but since both the parties declined Chandra Sekhar was invited to form the government and prove his majority in the House on or before 30 November 1990. Rajiv Gandhi kept his promise but Chandra Sekhar resigned out of ignominy on 6 March 1991 and advised dissolution of the Lok-Sabha. Thereafter on Rajib Gandhi's tragic assassination P.V. Narashima Rao was elected Leader of the Congress (I) parliamentary Party on 20 June 1991.[30]

It is unfortunate that the Chandra Sekhar Government's resignation made way for the 9th Government in Delhi since January, 1977 and, thus the average tenure of each government figured approximately one and half year only. Rao was however straight way appointed as Prime Minister on 20th June, but asked to establish his majority in the Lok-Sabha within four weeks. The motion of confidence was carried by 241 votes to 111. The National Front and the left abstained since none wanted fresh elections. Two years later Rao again was able to defeat a motion of no confidence by 265 to 251 with the support of the JMM members. It is true Rao managed to complete his tenure but subsequently he was convicted for indulging in corrupt practices using money power to manipulate a minority in the Lok-Sabha.[31]

In 1996's general election India again entered into the phase of Hung Parliament. The fact reveals that in the general election BJP bagged 161 seats in a house of 543 of which only 537 went to the polls. It won 20.7 per cent of the popular vote whereas allies promised another 34 seats with the Shiv Sena 15, the Akalis 8, the Samata Party 8 and the Haryana Vikas Party 3, the total number being 195 but fell short of magic figure of 269 by as many as 74. The BJP claimed to form a government on 11 May. President S.D. Sharma appointed A.B. Bajpayee as PM who was sworn in on 16 May. Mr. Bajpayee was advised to secure a vote of confidence by 31 May but assuming sure defeat in the Lok-Sabha Bajpayee announced his resignation on 28 May. Thereafter, H.D. Deve Gowda was appointed PM in June 1996 and secured a Vote of Confidence in the Lok-Sabha but could not survive beyond ten months because congress withdrew its support. It is queerest to note that Congress again extended support to I. K. Gujral as the new leader of the United Front and as such he was appointed PM. On 21 April with an instruction to seek a vote of confidence. On 28 November 1997, it was the same Congress(I) that declared its withdrawal of support to the government and did not fail to stake its claim to form the government.[32] This time unlikely Deve Gowda, Gujral resigned that very day but without advising dissolution of the Lok-Sabha.

In the 12th Lok Sabha of 1998, the ruling U.F. was defeated. The result shows: The BJP along with, its allies 252 whereas, the Congress and allies 166 and the UF's strength was 96. The president invited Vajpayee who was sworn in as PM on 10 March. This time, he won a vote of Confidence in the Lok-Shaba on 28 March by 274 to 261 but had not been allowed to servive beyond 13 months in office. Now, it was Sonia who held parleys with Jaylalita, Subramaniam Swami, Surjeet Singh, Jyoti Basu, Chandra Sekhar and Mulayam Singh who were the Prime architects of the grand design hatched to dislodge Mr. Vajpayee.[33]

After thirteen months, the verdict for the 13th Lok-Shaba was not unexpected and unusual. The result once again proved that India in its democratic journey has moved into a post Congress polity. This will be evident from the fact that the Congress had to be contented with 112 seats against 141 seats it won in 1998. The BJP 90 to 182 seats far less than the majority mark. In 1998 its tally was 178.[34] The trend is quite obvious that a fundamental restructuring of electoral politics is underway in the wake of the assertion of regional forces, viz., OBCS, dalits and minority communities. This is preventing any single party from dominating the electoral scheme in the country.

An analysis will show that the BJP led National Democratic Alliance with as many as 24 partners did well in those states where it had formed alliance with secular regional parties. Alliance has helped it to do better in the south and east of the country. In Tamil Nadu, the BJP got 7 seats and its partner TDP bagged 29 seats whereas in the Left dominated West Bengal, the BJP-Trinamul alliance got 10 out of 42 seats.[35] As regards, the Congress-led alliance with only five partners – AIADMK, KECM, MUL, RJD, and RLD, they secured only 134 seats. It is important to note that the Congress party expressed its relevance for a one party government equating coalition with instability. This approach is possibly based on a pragmatic understanding of the current dynamics of the electoral politics in India. The Nineties politics have shown that regional forces have emerged as significant players in Indian electoral structural pattern. The NDA is probably a sort of an experiment in federalism and coalition politics.

Reference, however, may be made in this context that in the 13th Lok-Shaba of the 70-odd members in Atal Behari Vajpayee's team several are unknowns. Of the known ones, few are old hands and some quite unsuitable. Mamata Benerjee wanted railways that do not in the opinion of politicians reduce the danger of an instinctive populist in charge of an organisation that needs trimming and reforms. She is likely to do a Paswan on railways.[36] The telecom sector is on the threshold of radical changes, and Paswan is about the worst choice to guide that transformation. Sharad Yadav slew Laloo Yadav, he could do the same to liberalised civil aviation. It is commonly felt that these and other lukewarm choices are the shamefully bloated size of Vajpayee's ministry. Many undesirables and incompetents would have been left out and the Prime Minister emerged stronger.

The recent exposure by *Tehelka Dot Com* is again a reminder that corruption is a terrible and endemic sickness of Indian Political life. It is undoubtedly, the most unfortunate fallout of the spy cam scandal that has caused the disruption of Parliament for nearly ten days. It has been reported that any discussion on railway and general budget's has been prevented. Thirty-five bills scheduled for introduction have been put on hold. Lok-Shaba activity has been reduced to rushing to the Well of the House and shouting slogans, one more tasteless than the other. If the Rajya Shaba has been better, probably no one has noticed. According to a quick estimate by experts over forty crores of taxpayers money has gone down the drain. A minister has been forced to explain his resignation in a television studio rather than before the national legislature. The leader of the opposition wants a similar slice of prime time and as such, has refused to let the two Houses meet unless the government puts in its papers. India's chosen politicians are making a collective spectacle of themselves[37]!

After *Tehelka*, the *Prevention of Terrorism Ordinance (POTO)* has sparked off angry discussions. Some opposition parties dubbed it a black law and are united in arms against the Ordinance just for the sake of narrow political gain. It is to be borne in mind that *POTO* is not the outcome of a sudden brainwave of the present government. The law commission in its report released in April 2000, felt the need for a special law to deal with the hydra-headed monster cross-border terrorism till April 2001 had taken a toll of 30,000 civilians, 5,101 security personnel and cost the exchequer around Rs.64,000 crores.[38] Whereas, the United Kingdom had enacted a similar anti-terrorist legislation following two bomb explosions in Birmingham pubs on 2nd November, 1974 and the 'Bill' was subjected to only two hours debate in the House of Commons and approved without a division[39]!

The fact cannot be denied that as BJP plays the Hindu card, the congress or the Marxist also play the religious card to woo Muslim voters even on issues which they know are not only out of the tune with their supposed brand of secular politics but what is also their avowed objective that is to combat communalism. For those who have looked up to them this has come as a major shock. Like bourgeois parties the Marxists take recourse to real politik. The result is a compromise with cherished ideals as the recent 'madrasa' issue has so sadly shown and consequent fall in their credibility. In support of the above argument reference may be made of the West Bengal Board of Madrasa Education act of 1994. It provides for a Board of 27 members, wholly under CPI (M) government control. It is interesting to note that no elections have ever been held, because government have not framed rules. There are 'High Madrasas', 'Junior Madrasas' and Madrasas; distinctions, inter se are obscure but all impart instraction in Arabic, Islamic history and culture and theology, 'senior madrasa' education includes Islamic jurisprudence or shariat law.[40]

It is known to all that the state government exercises total control under the act. The Board merely advises government. The Board's term is four years but indefinite extensions are permitted. The Board has a fund for contributions, fees, endowments and government grants, all to be recorded and section 26(d) provides that any other sums received by or on behalf of the Board from any source what so ever must be recorded.[41]

The Act is exhaustive and the state government also uses it brazenly to seek and retain Muslim votes. Government subventions keep registered madrasas afloat. It appears that between 1780 when the first madrasa came up, till 1977, there were 238 madrasas in total and after 1977, the Left Front formed the Board without legislative sanction and until 2002, the number of more than doubled to 507. The annual budget allocation at the end of congress rule was Rs. 570000; for 2000-01 it was Rs.115 crores[42]! It is thus evident that the madrasas are intended with a motive to produce vote for the CPI (M).

Of course, West Bengal Chief minister Mr. Buddhadev Bhattacharya made a factual and honest statement on 19th January. He conceded that unregistered madrasas need to be investigated particularly their sources of fund – Gulf money funnelled through Bangladesh.[43] He also added that some of them, who enjoy petro-dollar sponsorship, are not affiliated to the madrasa board and those investigations have begun with the corrupt ones. He also mentioned that he had specific information that illegal madrasas are carrying anti-national propaganda.[44]

The crisis brought about when the Imams in mosques threatened that their total support to the Left Front may be in danger because while during Jyoti Basu's tenure the two communities lived in amity but the situation changed after Mr. Bhattacharya took over the charge as Chief minister although the reality goes there is no evidence whatever that there has been any communal strike or other ugly manifestation of discontent. Now, several issues arise. Imams are religious leaders they have no business making political statements like expressing preferences for political leaders. This only gives a handle to communal elements among the Hindus to say – Muslims are not part of the main stream and they cannot be trusted. In fact, the Imams are doing no service to their own community. It is unfortunate that the statement of the Imam of Jama Masjid who eulogised Osama Bin Laden following 11th September and urged all good Muslims to go to Afghanistan to fight in the 'jihad'. Subsequently when Shabana Azmi delivered the 'bon mot' and asked government to fly the Imam to Afghanistan and drop him over Kandahar, he had no answer.

Imams are wrong to claim that madrasas are their private institutions; because they are not privately funded instead they are separately provided for in the state's education budget. The panic is over the discovery of a very large number of unregistered Madras as larger than even in Bangladesh are regularly funded by petro-dollars routed through that country.[45]

The period from 1995 to 2001 in West Bengal provided an interesting example of what has been referred to as 6.9 million bogus voters! The West Bengal Chief electoral officer Sabyasachi Sen's startling revelation that his enumerators struck off 69 lakh voters whose names should not have figured in the state electorals for last May's 13th assembly election. It is strange that repeated representations to the Chief Election Commission, President, Prime Minister, Governor and the Chief Electoral Officer himself to remedy the situation evoked no response. The most shocking part of the revised draft electoral roll is that instead of showing an increase in the number of voters which so far has been the case because of a 4 per cent average annual rise in the State's population, the Chief electoral officer says that there has been a 8 per cent full in the number of voters which in thoroughly unacceptable.[46]

The massive deletion of names vindicates the charge that the state's election machinery has been responsible for blatant fraud on the people. The question arises are West Bengal's porous borders responsible for the number of bogus voters in the state? The border districts in state have seen the inclusion of 80000 new voters. This is well above the average for the state. As for example Darjeeling, Cooch Behar, Jalpaiguri, Malda and Nadia districts have seen significant inclusions. Such a high figure of new entries in the electoral lists comes in the wake of repeated allegations by the opposition parties that the Left Front government was allowing infiltrators to settle in the border districts and providing them ration cards.[47]

An interesting aspect of the draft electoral rolls brought by the state election authorities is that not a single person got his or her name enlisted in the electoral of Midnapore West because of migration. In this district comprising areas of Midnapore and Kharagpur, 326840 persons have been described as "new entries to existing families". But there has not been a single entry in the voters list because of shifting. Midnapore west is the only such district in the state, suggesting no one to wants to move there; in the three Kolkata Lok Sabha constituencies only 116000 new voters as against a deletion of 666000 names of bogus voters.[48] It may be mentioned that Officials of Home Department of the government of the United Kingdom, who visited the NHRC in 1995, expressed the view that the police and security forces would not be able to checkmate the terrorists without a stringent anti-terrorist law. So, instead of trying to legitimise unpatriotic actions and glamorise the so-called 'vote bank' under parliamentary system the Indian political parties can learn a lesion or two from the British model and put the nation above petty politics.

The aforesaid analysis thus reveals that parliamentary democracy and especially the coalition politics is a costly adventure in the present political system of India. The Ministry being the result of coalition of several parties holding different views has no solid party support in the legislature. The reality is, coalition means many ministers and many ministers mean many compromises!

## References

1. Basu, D: Introduction to the Constitution of India, New Delhi, 1998 p. 50.
2. *Ibid.*
3. *Ibid.*
4. C. A. D. Vol. II p. 43.
5. AIR 1963 sc 1241 quoted in B.L. Hansaria's book: Does India need a new constitution? p. 24.

6. Hansaria, B. L: Does India need a new constitution? p. 25.
7. *Ibid.*
8. *Ibid.*
9. *Ibid.*
10. Basu, D: Comparitive federalism pp. 106-107.
11. Mukarji Nirmal and Arora Balveer: "Federalism in India: Origin and Development" quoted in B. L. Hansaria's book: Does India need a new constitution?
12. *Ibid.*
13. *Ibid.*
14. Basu, D: Introduction to the constitution of India 18 the edition, 1998 p. 395.
15. *Ibid* p. 396.
16. *Ibid* A critical survey of the 42nd Amendment, constitution al law of India, 1985.
17. Sinha, S. K.: Stemming the Rot; Change to Presidential System, The Statesman May 3, 1991.
18. Ghosh, D.: Presidential System only way, Calcutta 1991 p. 30.
19. *Ibid.*
20. *Ibid.*
21. *Ibid.*
22. *Ibid.*
23. Moddie, A.D.: The End of Dynasty; The Statesman September 10, 1993.
24. *Ibid.*
25. *Ibid.*
26. *Ibid.*
27. *Ibid.*
28. The Statesman, 27 April, 1999.
29. Ghose, D.: *Ibid.*
30. The Statesman, 27 April, 1999.
31. *Ibid* 30th September, 2000.
32. *Ibid.*
33. *Ibid.*
34. Behera, A. K.: Regions become equal partners The Statesman, 15 October, 1999.

35. *Ibid.*
36. The Statesman, 15 October, 1999.
37. India To-day, April 2, 2001.
38. The Statesman, 3 December, 2001.
39. *Ibid.*
40. The Statesman 10 February 2002.
41. *Ibid.*
42. *Ibid.*
43. *Ibid.*
44. *Ibid.*
45. The Sunday Statesman, Editorial, 10 February 2002.
46. *Ibid* 9 February 2002.
47. *Ibid* 11 February 2002.
48. *Ibid.*

# 5

# Should We Have The Parliamentary System?

"Good temper and moderation" wrote Thomas Erskine May, the mid 19th century authority on parliamentary practice, "are the characteristics of parliamentary language". What would this first baron of Farnborough and clerk of the House of Commons in the 1870's have made of Indian parliamentary behaviour to day? The question however, cannot really be asked in earnest. The fact is the Westminster model is what India started with. But imagining the baron in contemporary New Delhi could be a way of measuring the great distance the Indian houses have traversed from the letter and spirit of May's code of conduct.[1]

It is not that the English never play foul. Over two hundred years ago. Lord Sandwich told the radical John Wilkes that Wilkes would die upon the gallows or of the pox. "That depends, my lord". Wilkes replied, "on whether I first embrace your principles or your mistress". The labour leader, Mr Michael Foot, has likened Mr Norman Tebbit to a semi-house trained polecat", and Mr. Tony Banks, of same party had once said that Ms. Margaret Thatcher has the sensitivity of a sex-starved boa constrictor."[2] Expletives like squirt, twerp, fat bounder, pig's bladder and food mountain have been hurled across the floor. May also forbids cad, stoolpigeon, guttersnipe, swine and cheeky young pup. "Liar" is not allowed. So, Winston Churchill described somebody as having been economical with the truth. Such a long tradition of insult and abuse is of course, un-parliamentary. But it exists because of not in spite of an equally long tradition of lively but civilised debate, honoured and practiced by these masters of public insult. There is implicit here a shared political culture, a sense of decorum, which is sometimes robustly broken precisely because it is believed in, and shared.[3]

The fact cannot be denied that such a consensus as to what constitutes civilised behaviour in parliament or in the assembly has been utterly destroyed in India to-day. Reference may be made in this context that very recently Prime Minister Atal Behari Vajpayee admitted for the first time that he forced stiff challenge from a section of BJP MPs and VHP backed Sadhus in his effort to uphold the rule of law in Ayodhya. Without naming the MPs, Vajpayee said a pamphlet accusing him of "Hitlorshahi" (Hitlar's tyranny) was circulated inside and outside of parliament. "I want to ask one thing how can we not obey the constitution in its letter and spirit"? He asked, "They said they will not allow us to function as Hitlor. But who is Hitlor here"? Not only that Vajpayee referred to a letter sent to him by 14 Uttar Pradesh MPs who compared his government with the Fuehrer's 'tyranny' and demanded that the curbs in Ayodhya must be lifted immediately. Though most of these MPs were supposed to have participated in the Shila daan, they backed out once it appeared that the movement's spearheads – Ashoke Singhal and Ramchandra Das Paramhans – were in a conciliatory mood.[4] As a matter of fact, it appears that descended from Westminister, the Indian Parliament has lost the tradition of a shared and robust political culture.

As regards behavioural aspects of Parliamentary practice in India reference may be made that on 13th March 2002, their Lordships of the Supreme court Justices Kirpal, Patnaik and Khare expressed their displeasure at the spectacle of various counsel appearing for different parties in the Ayodhya imbroglio addressing them simultaneously instead of waiting their turn. They reminded Counsel that the Supreme Court was not Parliament and threatened to rise if they did not behave themselves. "The reference was not complimentary", says C.R. Irani to Parliament but can anyone say that the rebuke was not well-desired"[5]? He observes, "On an average day, in the Lok Sabha, the chances are that one will witesss a noisy walkout, parliamentarians will rush into the well of the House protesting their arguments often with fisticuffs to match and other misbehaviour.[6]

It is important to note that on occasion of the commemoration of Indian Parliament's Golden jubilee in 2002 it has been regretted that at the dawn of independence parliament converted itself into a constituent assembly to frame a constitution of which any country could be proud. It is contended that the debates of the proceedings handed down to us are a model of how parliament or any other legislative chamber purporting to express the people's will should function. It was possible to disgrace without danger to life and limb; debates influenced decisions, the art of argument was alive and well. And decisions arrived at were accepted as the collective wisdom of the House. Throughout it was treated as given that there was another point of view different form one's own, which was entitled to equal respect.[7]

It is also contended that as the parliamentary practice of today is contributing to its increasing irrelevance in the governance of the country it is matched by a growing concern for the well being of our politicians who are elected to the house. It has come to this that emoluments of members of parliament and the formidable list of perquisites grow in geometrical proportion to their importance. Members of parliament think nothing of voting themselves substantial increases at regular intervals even as they solemnly enjoin bet tightening on those they govern.[8]

The popular maxim goes that "counterfeit coins drive all good coins from the market; potentially able men and women in good conscience shun membership of parliament leaving the field for convicted offenders who know their way around the law courts to monopolise membership of the house to protect themselves. This is the reason why Laloo Prasad Yadav dubbed the Raja of Bihar, has decided to seek membership of the Rajya Sabha. Earlier, he ran Bihar like a fiefdom through his wife; he is more ambitious now – he will run Bihar from Delhi"[9]!

The same critic argues with documentary evidence that a particular handicap to good governance is parliamentary privileges. According to him parliamentary privileges are being used as a cloak and a device to avoid accountability at the very least. The constitution earlier provided that privileges would be the same as applied to the House of Commons in 1950. Indira Gandhi found this offensive to her notions of national honour. So she changed the form of words, not the substance. Privileges are now what they were at the date of commencement of the constitution. This brings us back to 1950 when privileges were, in any event those of the House of Commons, so nothing has changed because if suits members of Parliament to leave privileges undefined to be able to dangle the threat of being hauled up before the committee on privileges to avoid criticism.[10]

A concrete example may be cited in this context how freedom of speech and expression proceeds under an added peril. The fact goes that The Statesman reported that evidence led before the parliamentary committee investigating the scam in the US-64 scheme included that the much maligned P. Subramanyam who headed it spent two whole days with the Finance Minister in Delhi and the evidence of Secretary was that the Minister knew all about it. The Minister tried to talk his way out of it. He admitted to seeing Subramanyam but insisted that the later was only paying a courtesy call. It would not occur to a Minister, any minister, that such courtesy calls would be wasting the officials time because for contempt for public opinion runs deep. Caught behind the Minister seeks to deep freeze the issue by announcing that he has filed a privilege motion against the Statesman and its editor. It would be his hope that the motion would not be raised while he is still a Minister.[11]

Parliamentary democracy has been in operation since independence, both at the centre and the state. But during this period we cannot say that it has functioned smoothly and successfully. We already have seen in the foregoing chapter that the average life of a Chief Minister since the later half of the eighties is fifteen months and whereas, in the centre the I.K. Gujral government's resignation on 28 November, 1997 made way for the twelfth Government in Delhi since January, 1977 and thus the average life of Prime Minister becomes not more than nineteen months. Generally, Parliamentary system works best where there is a bi-party system and disciplined parties. Reference may be made in this context to the nature of successful working of the English system of parliamentary government about which Lord Bryce (1928) observes: "It presupposes the existence of two great parties and no more, parties each strong enough to restrain the violence of the other, yet one of them steadily preponderant in any given House of Commons, that where a third, perhaps a fourth, party appears, the conditions are changed and that the scales of Parliament oscillate as the weight of this detached group is thrown on one side or the other; dissolutions become more frequent, and even dissolutions may fail to restore stability.[12]

Walter Bagehot (1945), an eminent authority on the British constitution adds that parliamentary system of government provides for 'the fusion' of the executive power with the legislative power which means a continuous and concerted co-operation between the legislative and executive organs of a state and side by side the cabinet can compel legislation by the threat of resignation and the threat of dissolution, but neither of these can be used in a presidential state. There the legislature cannot be dissolved by the executive government and it does not heed a resignation for it has not to find the successor. Accordingly, when a difference of opinion arises, the legislature is forced to fight the executive, and the executive is forced to fight the legislative, and so very likely they contend to the conclusion of their respective terms.[13] Herman Finer (1950) substantially agrees with the views of Walter Bagehot. In a remarkably lucid style he says, "A seamless network holds together the Prime minister and the cabinet and the Parliament (in England). They are flesh of each others' flesh, in full sovereignty, for neither constitutional limitations nor courts declare them out of bounds, and they are still flesh of each others' flesh even when they are thorns in each others' flesh".[14] Moreover, by way of contrast, Sidney Low emphasizes that in the United States, the distinction of powers, theoretical with us, or obsolete, is still alive and operative. The Executive is kept apart from the legislature. The members of the cabinet do not sit in Congress, they are merely heads of departments, and responsible to the President who is the chief of the administration. Congress occupies itself in making laws and providing for the raising and disbursement of the Federal revenues. There is no ministry directly responsible to the legislature. It is further added that the American system divides responsibility and makes it difficult to place it anywhere whereas the Congress cannot control a President who has been elected without reference to its feelings and sympathies, for a fixed term of years; the President has no authority over a Congress which may happen to have a majority drawn from the party opposed to him, since he can not dissolve and appeal from the representatives to the electorate, and the House of Representatives has little power even over its own business, which is really transacted by the heads of the two-score little legislatures that owe their being to the speaker.[15] It is also to be noted that the above powers and responsibilities are supposed to be entrusted, under the true Cabinet system, to the same hands and they are exercised in an atmosphere of public discussion. They are combined in a governing council, which derives its existence from a representative chamber chosen directly by the electorate. The nation can be master in its own house; its energies can be directed along one channel instead of being dissipated by want of unity. The officers, the sailors, and the engineers of the ship of the state, can work in conjunction, with combined purpose and harmony of will. The House of Commons is theoretically strong, because it can call the Ministry to account for every act and compel their resignation by refusing supplies. The Ministry is its servant, but not its slave, for it can advise the king to dissolve parliament, appeal to the nation, and ask it to decide.[16]

Reference may also be made that Lord Balfour, while dealing with the British system of cabinet government observed that in England, the Prime Minister and his cabinet must co-operate or there would be no government. His Government and the House of Commons' majority which supports it must co-operate, or the Government must resign. Moreover, these needs are not unilateral, they are mutual. The party majority which refuses to support their leaders not only hamper a polarity which, be it good or bad, is that of their Government, but they probably injure their own electoral prospects.

Leaders who refuse to work together not only weaken their cabinet and their party, but probably do little to strengthen their own political position. An administration whose policy unduly strains the loyalty of any large section of its supporters is obviously making things easy for its opponents.[17]

Professor Laski (1949) concludes that an executive who cannot command the confidence of the legislature may appeal beyond it to the electorate. So long as it controls the legislature, its authority is coherent and integrated. These are immense advantages. The authority may be abused, but at least, the responsibility for the abuse is always clearly indicated. The energy of the executive is not continually dissipated in patching up the majorities it requires for some degree of the programme it has urged. The allegiance of its supporters is not constantly shifting on its axis. There is not a continuous interest in the legislature to develop a policy of its own at the cost of executive credit, the modern state requires disciplined leadership but the American system leaves no assurance of its continuous availability.[18]

No doubt, the above conditions for successful working of parliamentary system are not present in the structural pattern of political parties in India. Empirical knowledge of the working of the party system in India since independence leads us to the fact that from 1947 to 1967 there was one party dominant system (The Indian National Congress) with a tendency to bend parliamentary institutions to its needs and from 1967 till present-time phase is characterised as instability and uneasy transition to multi-party situation which necessitated the formation of coalitions proved fragile leading to political instability.

Referring to the system of parliamentary practice in India, Madhok (1993) emphasizes that in India, partition resulted from the mixing of religion and politics by the Muslim League in keeping with the Islamic tradition but unfortunately such communal party was not only allowed to be revived but was also given new respectability by making it coalition partner in the government of Kerala both by the Congress and the Communist parties.[19] He also added, "Nehru created among the Muslims who had not left for Pakistan a fear psychosis and projected himself as their saviour to ensure a dependable Muslim vote bank for his party in future democratic elections.[20]

Lord Balfour agrees with the views of Walter Bagehot that the homogeneity of the people and a national outlook are the strong foundations on which parliamentary democracy stands. But unfortunately, in spite of the fact that castism in the traditional sense is weakening in India and though the leaders of our country have proclaimed that caste is a menace to our national life, caste plays a significant role in Indian politics and particularly in regional or state politics. Adult Franchise and Panchayati Raj have given new opportunities to castes. Numerically large castes have become important pressure groups in politics in the state and district levels. Dr. Leach aptly remarks: Everywhere in India and Ceylon to-day whole caste groups are tending to emerge as political factions.[21]

People at village level cultivate ministers for favours and privileges and ministers also in their turn need the help of village leaders during elections. Moreover, "Many, if not most ministers" remarks Srinivas, are also leaders of their own castes and through this of their region also. Surprisingly, voters do not even understand that it is not right to demand that the elected minister help his caste-folk.[22] As for example, in Mysore state politics, there is a traditional rivalry between Okkaligas and Lingayats, the two leading peasant castes. In Kerala, there is a triangular struggle between Nayars, Izhavans and Syrian Christians and where as, in Andhrapradesh the Chief contesting castes are Reddis and Kamonas in Maharastra, Brahmans and Mohar; in Gujrat, Baniyas, Patidars and Kolis and in Bihar, Bhumidar, Kaystha and Rajput.[23]

In 1952 election, it was believed that the congress party in Madras was pursuing in the spheres of education and recruitment to services a policy which meets with support from Dravida Kazhagam. It is also to be noted that the success of the congress in Madras was partly attributed to its pursuing a policy which mode a non-Brahmin party and subsequently Dravida Munnetra Kazhagam (DMK) came into being as a non-Bbrahmin Party to break the Brahmanical dominance in Madras state Politics.[24] During the same year, in the election, the Communist party of India supported Dravida Kazhagam candidates while in 1967's election the CPI (M) joined hands with DMK party in order to defeat the congress.[25] Again, in Bihar during the 1951-52 election strong caste principals followed in Congress party. As for example, the Rajputs were led by the then Food Minister Shri A. N. Sinha and the Bhumidars were led by the then Chief Minister Dr. Srikrishna Sinha whereas Shri K.B. Sahay, Minister for Revenue and Excise led the Kayasthas. Interestingly, in defiance of party loyality Rajputs supported Rajput nominees and many Kayasthas supported their caste fellows. The Congress party exploited the principle of caste politics in the elections, the traditional caste rivalry in the Bihar Congress has not ceased even today and it is believed to be one of the reasons for the disintegration of party leadership in that state.

Similar cases are avilable in Uttarpradesh. Shri Jai Ram Varma who was agricultural minister during 1970's had related a kind of 'Kurmi' political 'Jati' in Faizabad district which had provided him with an indestructible political base for more than thirty years.[26] Similar instance may be cited in respect of Sri Jagjiban Ram who as the leader of the Scheduled castes had been able to occupy a permanent place in the Cabinet of the Indian union. The Caste policy in Haryana is not less interesting. In November 1967, the Jat leaders joined hands with the Brahmin leader Sri Bhagawat Dayal to bring down the Ahir-led ministry of Rao Birendra singh. In December 1968, the Congress Ministry in Haryana faced a critical situation, which was described by Link (Indian Weekly) as Ahir-Brahman revolt against the Jats.[27]

Besides, many castes associations had been started in almost all big towns of the Country in imitation of political parties. As for example; the conference of all India Jadava Maha Sabha is a case in point. The Conference was organised purely on the basis of castism but class interest and class relations were also dominant.

This will be evident from the speech of Rao Birendev Singh, the President of the Maha Sabha which points out that the aim of the Maha Sabha is among others, to establish a popular government of 'Kisans' to put on end to the monopoly of Banias.[28] The above cases are almost throughout, India sufficiently substantiate the fact that castism influences political activity from the Panchayat right up to parliamentary election. It is true that with the advancement of modernity castismn is losing its importance but it is also true that conflicts between castes are, being manipulated by political criminals. All political parties even Marxists are not free from prejudices even after the spar of more than fifty years since independence.

In England or America hardly a life is lost in the election campaign, during which opposing contestants address newsmen and the voters from the same platform presenting alternative programme to solve the same national problems, from which the electorate can make their choice for a new Government but reversely, in India, on the other hand, it has become a common practice that when a political leader is determined to win an election at any cost he has to use younger people as tools in his election campaign of bloodshed.[29] What excites us very much is the report of a chief minister entering jail on a criminal charge deputing his wife to carry on his work.[30]

Very recently, Mr. Saifuddin Chowdhury, a rebel CPI (M) leader of West Bengal without going for any direct confrontation with the party said, "a thorough probe was needed to find out why peace has suddenly been replaced by violence after twenty-three years of left front rule, but one thing is clear there are many options other than violence to counter violence.[31]

The purport of Mr. Chowdhury's speech was somewhat at variance with the party's explanation that the violence in the strife-torn districts or Midnapur, Bankura and Hooghly of West Bengal was the outcome of 'reign of terror' by Trinamul Congress led by Ms. Mamata Benerjee. Echoing the party's view, someone concluded, violence restored to for ending terror like the one in Vietnam is something holy.[32]

The trend of violence is not less serious in the case of Tamil Nadu. It is quite known to all that Ms. Jayalalitha's nomination papers for the elections were rejected on the ground that she was a convicted criminal and was barred under section 8 of the Representation of the People Act. At the head of a victorious party she nevertheless got herself sworn in by the Governor in double quick time, who, let it be noted, was once a Supreme Court Judge and must be presumed to understand the basic principles of representative government even if she cannot claim to be expert on constitutional norms. Her request to Jayalalitha to wait for a day while she got advice was answered by a peremptory demand to be made chief minister at once. The Governor complied. It is incomprehensible that an effective legal challenge to the series of illegalities was not immediately mounted and that the Union Government felt so utterly helpless as to do nothing. Delhi's curious inaction led to speculation that the BJP were eying Jayalalitha's MPs significantly more numerous that what Mamata Banerjee could muster, if the 'number game' became crucial for the survival of the Vajpayee administration. The result was the barbarity.[33] At dead of night of 30th July, 2001 policemen barged into the home of former chief minister M. Karunanidhi and dragged him out of bed and down the steps of his house screaming his head off and bundled him into a policeman vehicle tearing his cloths in the process. Two central ministers who tried to intervene got beaten up and were not allowed to accompany Karunanidhi. The Governor who was asked for a full report sent a two-page note, which should be presented as an illustration of how to confuse and condone. There was no warrant of arrest and no notice to the accused. In fact, vulgarity and abuse of power had lent a new dimension to polluted political culture.[34]

This sort of violent political culture has no place in parliamentary democracy and it needs to be corrected by the reorientation of approach among the people.

Political realists believe that a system of government is like a tool or a human hand. What is relevant is the temperament, shaped by history, and the mind using it. The human hand both kills man and creates works of art and literature. For the British the Westminster system has worked. Even in British India, under the Government of India act of 1935; at least on restricted franchise, the Westminister system worked. But the Indian psyche and tradition, according to the undisputed allegations of a Prime Minister and his Finance Minister holding office, have converted the Westminster system into a chamber for "horse trading" and a "game of numbers" stalemating the administration and endangering public good.[35] It is however, true that in the closing stage of Nehru's India people started talking about the grave rise in corruption in everyday life and as a remedial measure G.H.Nanda, the then Home minister set up "Sadachar Samities" in every state but to little or no avail.[36] Now a days, there is hardly any talk about corruption but more and more people in the Corridors of power talk these days about the criminals, economic offenders and the under world kings succeeded in many instances indirectly or directly establishing access to citadels of power including political parties.

In certain instances Ghose (1991) observes: The threat by economic interest group to the Government made through the ruling party's base and consequently the pressure of economic interest groups and MLAs / MPs act as the proverbial Sword of Damocles on the head of the Government.[37] In fact, this is a total gist picture of India's west minister experience. It is now an open secret that to both survive and prosper, economic offenders find refuge among big economic interest groups and so-called politicians. Not only that, often the substantial social welfare work participation of economic offenders makes for greater acceptance socially and professional acceptance certainly.[38] A more fundamental cause of the trend towards the failure of Parliamentary democracy is probably the narrow- mindedness and selfishness of the representatives of the people who shamelessly illustrated when on the last day of sitting of the Ninth Lok –Sabha, the MPs unanimously voted for ensuring their pension, and at an enhanced rate, even though the Lok-Sabha was dissolved after a short duration, without caring to see that a bill or motion having financial liability could not be introduced without the President's recommendation (Art. 117(1) of the constitution).

It is paradoxical when Jyoti Basu remarks that the recent move for pay hike for MPs (300 percent in salaries, which will cost the exchequer about Rs. 23.778 crores!) and the handsome increase in their perks and other benefits. He should however be welcomed by all since there has been a popular backlash to the largesse that self-indulgent MPs want to shower on themselves. But should someone like Jyoti Basu, whose preaching and practices have vastly differed be sermonising on issues like morality and ethics? It is reported that on the eve of stepping down from Chief ministership, he did not even care to set up a committee to recommend the benefits that he and other former Chief ministers should get during retirement. In fact, what was done in the name of providing benefits including security and protection to this octogenarian patriarch forms one of the most sordid Chapters of misuse of power and authority.[39]

It is interesting to note in this context that when Mr. Buta Singh was convicted along with others for indulging in corrupt practices in the Jharkhand Mukti Morcha bribery case on 29 September 2000, Mr. Singh somewhat unashamedly proclaimed. "I did it for the party".[40] It was obvious that Mr. Singh meant that there was nothing very wrong in what had happened to him as long as the conviction was for corrupt practices committed by him for the sake of party. He had the courage to do or say so, because he knew that politicians like him are in great demand these days. Even the BJP had no compunction in taking his support for forming the government at the centre and inducting into the cabinet some time back, knowing fully well the serious charges of corruption that Buta Singh was facing, although his appeal against the charges at the time were pending in the Supreme Court. It was unfortunate that though the former Prime Minister P.V. Narshima Rao and Buta Singh were found guilty of entering into a criminal conspiracy between themselves and others to abet members of Parliament belonging to Jharkhand Mukti Morcha – Suraj Mandal, Shibu Soren, Simon Marandi and Sailendra Mahato – to accept bribes for extending support to the Congress (I) government in the Lok Sabha on 28 July, 1993. Others including Ajit Singh, Bhajan Lal, Satish Sharma facing charges in the same bribery case were acquitted, not honourably but for lack of evidence. Mr. N.K. Singh, a former CBI officer observed, "In fact, nothing better can be expected from an investigating agency when the Head of government and his cabinet colleagues are on a spree to purchase members of Parliament to survive in power. Luckily, the investigation fell into the hands of capable, conscientious and dedicated CBI officers who did a good job of it and submitted altogether three charge-sheets, the last being on 22nd January 1997 in good speed by any standards".[41] The fact goes that they were hauled up for charges like bribing members of the Parliament and accepting bribe and the court of law had framed charges against them for trial on the basis of prima facie evidence should have made them hang their heads in shame. But it was merely a reflector of standards in public life in the country to-day and the levels to which it has sunk.[42]

A.G. Noorani (1997) rightly states that the constitutions of India, Pakistan and Sri Lanka provide against the vice of defections testifies to the state of political morality in South Asia. The defector is not a dissident who crosses the floor of the House out of honest conviction. He is a political prostitute who sells his party membership for a price; the adversary who procures his services, thus in order to acquire power for himself, is no less guilty.[43]

It is interesting to note that B. K. Nehru in his memoirs narrates graphic and authoritive account of one such exercise in Kashmir in 1984: "The standard rate" for each of the 13 MLAs needed as defectors in order to topple Farooq Abdullah's Ministry, "was two lakh rupees in cash and a ministership. The funds were provided by my friend Tirath Ram Amla, a staunch and tried congress worker, and were supplied to him in cash from congress money in Delhi, transported in the mail pouches of the intelligence Bureau".[44] He adds: Since the events related in my story, this rate has far outstripped the rate of inflation".[45]

It is more amusing to note that President Zail Singh told Nehru that a lakh would have sufficed. When told it was not enough, "he said rather disgustedly, .... Yes, that Bhajan Lal has spoilt the rate".[46] The job was done to placate the presiding deity of the day, Indira Gandhi, who of course had no qualms about resort to unethical means nor had Rajib Gandhi. The law he rushed through in January 1985 was designed to freeze his majority. It deters individual defectors but permits wholesale trading.[47]

Charges of corruption and serious criminal records have almost ceased to be 'taboo' in public life and are very fast acquiring acceptability. Options for the general public are getting limited, thanks to such practices becoming endemic. This is in fact the greatest danger facing Indian, Parliamentary democracy today. We tried to fight so-called "Jungle Raj" of Laloo Prasad Yadav in Bihar, set up with the help of and collaboration with known criminals and mafia dons in the recent assembly elections in Bihar. Luckily, the general public are also becoming discerning. We know what happened in the assembly elections. This therefore holds out some hope for the future.[48]

It is therefore, widely felt that this is not in Parliamentary democracy but its 'death-knell' and if something is not done immediately, the future generations will place a big question mark on our national leaders by reference to Karl Marks, "The Eighteenth Brumaire of Louise Bonaparte", about the bride being brought home, but only after she had become a whore.[49]

Besides the above realities, the combination of federalism and the Parliamentary form of government poses some serious problems. For example, the basic Philosophy of federalism generates decentralising tendencies, whereas, the philosophy of parliamentary system re-enforces centralising tendency. Secondly, federal system are the outcome of evaluation of the governance of the people in heterogeneous, diverse and plural society inhabiting vast land tracts, while the parliamentary system is basically for governance of a homogenous people in a small country. Finally, the stresses and strains are likely between the head of the state and Head of the government, because the former is called upon to act in a dual capacity.

The question naturally arises why was parliamentary form of government was chosen? To answer the above question reference may be made that at the time of framing of the constitution, Dr Ambedkar said: "A democratic executive must satisfy two conditions: (1) it must be a stable executive and (2) it must be a responsible executive. Unfortunately, it has not been possible so far to devise a system, which can ensure both in equal degree. You can have a system which can give you more stability but less responsibility or you can have a system which gives more responsibility but less stability. The American and the Swiss systems give more stability but less responsibility. The British system on the other hand gives you more responsibility but less stability. The reason for this is obvious. The American executive is a non-parliamentary executive which means that it is not dependent for its existence upon a majority in the congress as the congress of United States cannot dismiss the executive while the British system is a parliamentary executive. A parliamentary government must resign the moment it loses the confidence of a majority of the members of Parliament. Looking at it from the point of view of responsibility, parliamentary executive being dependent upon a majority in parliament becomes more responsible. The parliamentary system differs from a non-parliamentary system in as much as the former is more responsible than the latter but they also differ as to the time and agency for assessment of their responsibility. Under the non-parliamentary system such as the one that exists in the USA the assessment of the responsibility of the executive is periodic. It takes place once in two years. It is done by the electorate. In England where the Parliamentary system prevails, the assessment of responsibility of the executive is both daily and periodic. The daily assessment is done by the members of parliament through questions, resolutions, no-confidence motions, adjournment motions, and debates on addresses, periodic assessment is done by electorate at the time of election which may take place every five years or earlier. The daily assessment of responsibility, which is not available under the American system, is, it is felt far more effective than the periodic assessment and far more necessary in a country like India. The draft constitution in recommending the parliamentary system of executive has preferred more responsibility to more stability.[50]

K.M. Pannikar who had stated in this regard had dealt with the aforesaid issue: "The structure of parliamentary democracy had been reared in India on a solid foundation for over a period of hundred years. India did not start on her democratic career on the date of her independence. She had travelled along the road for a considerable distance and it was impossible for her to retrace steps".[51]

Thus it appears that the constituent assembly was merely culmination of a process and evaluation which had commenced under the British rule and passed through several stages of development. The present constitution was thus carried strictly from the Government of India act 1935. Another reason assigned is that the dedicated Indians had come to imbibe the ideas and ideals of Western liberal democracy nurtured as they had been in the political philosophy of Burke, Mill and Dicey. The result was that our political leaders had come to look upon Westminister model as the goal of their constitutional aspirations and so it was little surprising that when the time came for them to exercise the choice they opted in favour of this model. This has been assigned as a reason of being absence of any impassionate impartial and objective debate or discussion regarding the system of government to be adopted.[52]

Now, to think that India's present constitution is designed to recreate the "British Parliamentary System" in the country is a grievous error. The British always had two systems; one for themselves, and the other for the colonies. Our constitution definitely belongs to the latter category and contains all the features against which the American Revolution started in 1776. It is unfortunate that we minimise the importance of American Revolution in the history and its relevance to India. Much of democracy as we know and practice in the modern world owes its origin to the American Revolution which broke the spine of world wide oligarchy and established the idea of republicanism in independent dignified nation states. American Revolution in 1776, followed by the French Revolution in 1789 and more recently by Russian Revolution in 1917 finally disabled imperialism and had the likes of the British packing for home. In fact the British have never played any role in promoting democracy anywhere in the world, leave alone India.[53]

Under the present parliamentary system, the unelected persons, as "yaars" and "dosts" of the ruling elite, are superior to the ones elected by the people. For example, an unelected person can become a Prime Minister, a Chief Minister, and certainly be a Governor. As a Governor either he or she has the power and the audacity to dismiss everyone who has been elected by the people. Witness Bhandaris in U.P. or Kants in Andhra. Can we call it the British system of parliamentary form of government? Do the British have anything like an unelected Governor who can dismiss the elected representatives of the people[54]? No. The British may have left India in a technical sense, but the constitutional system ensures that for the average Indian the British rule never ended in reality. Not only that the system has been used to divide the people on the basis of caste, language, religion and domicile. Scholars worldwide rightly describe as the Government sponsored caste system in the name of reservation!

In this context, the observation of Durga Das Basu, (1998) the leading constitutional writer is important. He says: three reasons for our cabinet system of Government having not worked as successfully as in England are:

(1) We have got in system of multiple parties, some of which are of mushroom growth or have an insignificant body of followers;

(2) very few of these parties have any firm or defined policy or ideology which can be presented as an alternative to that advocated by the party in power and

(3) the tradition of the party system in India has been destructive, because of its origin in the upsurge against the imperial rule of which destruction was the principal weapon. Therefore, even after the attainment of independence, some of the parties wasted much time and energy in asserting that this independence was not real, instead of educating themselves in running the administration, which has become not only an art but also a science in modern times.[55]

Thus, thoughts cannot but turn to the long mooted proposal of the present Westminster model's replacement by a new system of Government installing a stronger and more effective executive against economic offenders, committed to act independently of pressure groups and without fear or favour complete its fixed tenure quite unaffected by the loss of legislature support and only at that end of the tenure, accountability remains to the voter.

## References

1. The Telegraph Editorial, 17, March 2002.
2. The Telegraph, 17, March 2002.
3. *Ibid.*
4. *Ibid.*
5. C. R. Irani: Parliament – an editor's view (The Statesman 16 July 2002.
6. *Ibid.*
7. *Ibid.*
8. *Ibid.*
9. *Ibid.*
10. *Ibid.*
11. *Ibid.*

12. Lord Bryce: The American Commonwealth Vol. I. 1928 p. 288.
13. Walter Bagehot: The English Constitution, Oxford, 1945, p. 12.
14. Herman Finer: The theory and practice of Modern Government, 1950 p. 697.
15. Sidey Low: The Government of England, 1919 pp. 15-16.
16. *Ibid.*
17. Banerjee, D. N.: Some-Aspects of the Indian Constitution pp. 17-18.
18. H. Laski: The American Democracy; A commentary and interpretation, 1949 pp.72- 77.
19. The Statesman, Sept. 02, 1993.
20. *Ibid.*
21. *Ibid.*
22. Bhattacharya, D. C: Sociology p. 437.
23. Srinivas, M. N.: Caste in Modern India quoted in D. C. Bhattacharya's Sociology p. 437.
24. Bhattacharya, D. C.: Sociology.
25. *Ibid.*
26. *Ibid.*
27. *Ibid.*
28. *Ibid.*
29. Basu, D.: Introduction to the Constitution of India, 1998 p. 417.
30. The Statesman.
31. *Ibid.*
32. The Statesman, 23rd September, 2000.
33. The Statesman 2 July, 2001.
34. *Ibid.*
35. Ghose, D.: Presidential system only way, 1991 Preface.
36. *Ibid.*
37. *Ibid.*
38. *Ibid.*
39. The Statesman (Editorial) 27 August 2001.

40. Basu, D.: p. 417.
41. The Statesman 8, Nov, 2000.
42. Ghose, D: Presidential system only way pp. 18-148.
43. Noorani, A. G.: Vice of Defections-I published in the Statesman, 4 September 1997.
44. *Ibid.*
45. *Ibid.*
46. *Ibid.*
47. *Ibid.*
48. Constitution Assembly Debates Vol. VII, pp. 32-33.
49. Hansaria, B. L.: Does India needs a new constitution? p. 8.
50. *Ibid.*
51. *Ibid.*
52. *Ibid.*
53. Deb Sharma, K: What constitutes India? Published in the Statesman, 24 May 1998.
54. *Ibid.*
55. Basu, D.: Introduction to the constitution of India (1998) p. 417.

# 6

# Pertinence To Presidential System

In the thirteenth Lok-Sabha of the seventy odd members in Mr. Atal Behari Vajpayee's team Several were unknown, and of the known ones, few were old hands and some quite unsuitable and roles of most of the thirty seven ministers of state remained undefined, while some continued to hunt for spaces in the ministry, others were told to keep their mouth shut and simply enjoy being ministers. It was over a month after Mr. Vajpayee's ministry sworn in, the scathing remark about the team in the media was "all perk and no work in the Vajpayee jumbo team".[1] The above picture is not exceptional to the state cabinets rather the irreducible fall-out of coalition politics.

The Sarkaria commission recommended that the council of ministers should not exceed 10 per cent of the strength of the Assembly or Parliament.[2] This is followed more in the breach than the observance. There is, of course, a sound logic to the recommendation. The Government spends a large amount of money on the upkeep of ministers. And this is an unconscionable burden on the public exchequer. It is a general fact that small ministries mean valuable resources saved and our country, which has been on the brink of pauperisation, any saving of public money is greatly to be desired. That is the solid argument against huge unwieldy ministerial teams. It is interesting to note that now a day, a novel formula is adopted. As for instance, MLAs with two terms behind them are to get full cabinet status; those with one term get to be ministers of state. Newcomers to the assembly will be inducted into the ministry later. The farcical has been the staple of present day politics.[3] This formula, however, defies comprehension. By elementary logic, selection of ministers and the allocation of portfolios are based on political considerations based on factors like factional balance (in a single-party majority Scenario) and ideally, judgement about competence and temperament.

In fact, we are very close to the destabilization of the decades of the 1970's, 1980's and 1990's to realise that India is dazed and benumbed. All the media including 'Doordarshan' and 'Akash-vani' continuously providing news of the elites condemning the criminalization of politics and even some MPs are on record stating on the floor of the House that "Muscle power and money power are depriving the voter of the right to vote". Mention may be made here that the former Prime minister, Mr. P.V. Narasimha Rao, and his cabinet colleague, Mr. Buta Singh have been convicted in JMM MPs' bribery case. They have been found guilty under section 120-B (criminal Conspiracy) of the Indian Penal code.[4] The story began with a no-confidence motion in the Lok-Sabha in July, 1993 when Mr. Rao's minority congress survived but interestingly the counsel for Mr Narasimha Rao in the Jharkhand Mukti Morcha case provided novel arguments to keep his client out of jail. His argument was even assuming there was an offence of bribery committed, the act was performed within the precincts of Parliament and therefore beyond the reach of the Courts. The council also argued that even assuming that the offence of bribery was in fact committed, it was to achieve a "legitimate end" that is to say, the survival of his government. He urged that Article 75 (3) of the constitution "makes it mandatory for a Prime minister facing a no-confidence motion to save his government." But the Article in question says, "The Council of Ministers shall be collectively responsible to the House of the people".[5] Hence, it does not follow that a minister is not responsible for his actions under the ordinary law. A Prime Minister is also under no compelling constitutional obligation to save his government, he can give way, or can force a division, it is absurd to suggest that he is under a duty to stop at nothing, not even the commissioning of an offence, to stay in office. It is quite wrong to elevate a crude instinct for survival into a constitutional obligation.[6]

It is unfortunate that with the aid and abetment of the Westminster system and its game of numbers admissible in it, certain sections of the rural land power, thrust on Nehru's economic policy, which included grant of food grains business and pricing to rural land power. They keep raising the prices because they make big donations to all political parties. It is almost an open secret that a section of rural land power has institutionalised hoarding and illegal profiteering.[7] Not only that in the industrial front too economic interests group have thrust policy mistakes on successive governments in Delhi with the aid of the British Westminster model and the game of numbers admissible in it. The watershed in free Indian's industrial history is the 1956-61 second Five year plan period, which according to a number of Scholars, is a "Jerky uneven type of deficit financing" and that is, greatly responsible even for to-day's huge unaccounted (black money) money in circulation reaching the monstrous level of a parallel economy of Forty thousand crores disrupting totally intelligent and coordinated effort at controlling the economy and upsetting all calculations.[8] Ghosh (91) reiterates that this "Jerky" type of deficit financing was undertaken by the central Government under pressure from certain economic interest groups with total disregard for safeguards against deficit financing like higher production and simultaneous promotion of wage goods industry suggested duly by the Central Government's senior administration, but ignored and overruled by the political masters.[9] It is disgraceful to note that at present India is one of the World's most corrupt countries. The six Annual International corruption perception Index prepared by Transparency International, an international NGO based in Berlin and which released it on 15 September, 2000 have placed India 69th among 90 countries. The fact that the latest index gave India 2.8 on a scale of ten as against 2.9 last year means that in international perception corruption has increased in India.[10] This degeneration has seriously affected the Vitality of all our Political institutions including the legislature. To-day, both at the Centre and the States, legislature no longer reflects the will of the people, but only the iron will of government or, for that matter, of the ruling party: it is not any more a Daniel to give its judgements on issues and politics affecting the nation, but only a forum to transmit to the people "His Master's voice". It all started when Indira Gandhi, taking advantage of the internal emergency, made the Indian parliament her domestic handmaid and forced it to do many things which any legislature conscious of its authority and dignity would never have done. The Story, at the level of the

Indian states is not much different and even West Bengal under Left rule is no exception in this matter. It is unfortunate that during the last several years the Sessions of the West Bengal Legislative Assembly have been getting shorter and shorter reflecting the attitude of the government that it itself is the real guardian of the people and the task of the legislature is merely to follow its dictates. The report goes that in West Bengal, in the name of local self-government, there has been a heavy cut in the powers and functions of the MLAs outside the Assembly. This is, surely an open insult to the authority of the legislature.[11]

As regards the state of lawlessness, the state of Bihar probably tops the list. Here, the police stations are on perpetual holiday. Men in uniform in Mr. Laloo Prasad Yadav's fiefdom make it a point to be absent just when they are most needed. Private armies of landlords go on a killing spree with no questions asked and no punishment administrated. It becomes worse when hordes of musclemen in the grab of Yuba Janata Dal activists force their way into the Rajdhani Express at Patna to attend a rally in the Capital because their: own government at the centre needs them. The Chief Minister's silence on what has been happening suggests that he considers the events normal. His preoccupations as Janata Dal president blind him to the steady manifestation of Jungle law where ruler and the ruled are partners in crime. The single most encouraging development has been crackdown by the CBI on senior policemen. A section of IPS officers are alleged to have made a fast buck through purchase of inferior uniforms. Of course, this is nothing beside the startling revelation in a Police report that the names of 20,000 Police constables exist in departmental registers drawing salaries and other entitlements while they actually work in farms and houses of senior Police officers so far away from their actual place or posting that they cannot be traced – a stroke of inventive genius hard to beat. Any thing goes in Bihar where scams are for the asking but someone must wake up to the fact that the administration is playing with the lives of millions of citizens.[12] It is lamentable that at present political leadership of national stature has become scarce. Ministers lack both competence and experience to deal with national issues. Instead of dealing with national issues they dabble in local politics. Again, a sense of idealism has disappeared from public life. Ministers and others holding political power tend to make a fast buck. Ideals of service and sacrifice have given way to the masked pursuit of self-interest.

Nobody appears to be above suspicion and not even the Prime minister is an exception. In the largest democracy in the world of to day, one corrupt party is voted out of power only to be succeeded by another party, which is no less corrupt. The inflation of prices finds its immortal counterpart in the inflation of corruption while a weak and unstable government contributes to the erosion of discipline.

Five decades after the end of the British rule in India, probably we have lost enough time to take stock of the present situation. However, even now we can think to the kind of future that India must strive to build up. We already have discerned that our country has moved from corruption in the closing Nehru years of 1963-64 to the growing influence and power of criminals and economic offenders on our public life in this millennium with the apprehension of grave danger to economic freedom and political sovereignty.[13] Obviously, the question arises, how can we set the wrongs right? Surely, solution cannot be sought in frequent general elections which are expensive both in terms of money and unproductive energy, beyond the means of poor country like India and moreover, there is no guarantee of a return to conditions of Political health and stability. Some political pundits out of despair seek solution in the idea of dictatorship. In this respect, Prof. Datta (1997) writes in his article, India To-day, "this can be a remedy worse than the disease". Pakistan and Bangladesh have experimented with dictatorship. It has failed to produce their conditions of Political stability. Nor is dictatorship immune from corruption. Power corrupts Nigeria and Pakistan; two dictatorship countries have ranked lowest in an international corruption perception index. For India, with its great ethnic diversity, the straitjacket of dictatorship would be particularly inappropriate. Our experiment must retain the basis of democracy even when we introduce innovative forms.[14]

After all, whatever the solution might be, definitely, it is not lying with the west minister system, which however good and however strong a Government is in New Delhi, it will inevitably be felled by the "game of numbers" and "horse trading". It is therefore, a structural change is necessary as a guarantee of completion of a Government's tenure with of course, the legislature's power to reject proposal or bill presented by the Government. This particular structure is probably provided for by the Presidential system.

Mention may be made in this context that on October 27, 1984, the press club of Calcutta organised a panel discussion on "The Presidential system of Government" with the distinguished personalities like Asoke Sen, Vasant Sathe, and Justice Krishna Iyer. Somnath Chatterjee, Snehangshu Acharjee, Bhola Sen, etc. Mr. Deepankar Ghosh, the moderator of the panel discussion started by recounting what had been said in favour of and against the Presidential System of Government on the day of panel discussion. The contention of the opposition parties that the proposed Presidential system of Government was "a cover for excessive Centralisation endangering public good" was mentioned. The moderator also placed on record the stand of Mr. Sathe and other stalwarts endorsing his views that the public purpose would be best served if a system could be revolved that would ensure two aspects of government, viz., the power of the legislature to reject the executive's proposal and the right of the executive to continue in office for its full term, despite losing the legislature's support, as in the united states of America and France. Mr. Sathe advocated the amendment to articles 54 and 55 (Art. 54 says: "The president shall be elected by the members of an electoral college consisting of – (a) the elected members of both Houses of Parliament and (b) the elected members of the Legislative assemblies of the States," and Art. 55: (1) As far as practicable, there shall be Uniformity in the Scale of representation of the different States at election of the President (2) For the purpose of securing such uniformity among the states inter se as well as parity between the states as a whole and the Union, the number of votes which each elected number of Parliament and of the Legislative Assembly of each state is entitled to at such election shall be determined.[15])

Mr. Sathe made it clear that he advocated no departure from the broad West Minister model of Government that worked in this country. But Mr. Justice Krishna Iyer contended that risks were involved in having a direct election of the President by the people through amendments to Articles 54 and 55. Because, a President elected by the People could bring himself to challenge the powers of the Prime Minister and the Lok-Sabha; such an eventuality could never ensure stability. He also felt that the amendments only to Articles 54 and 55 would not serve the purpose of ensuring a more powerful President and those amendments to articles 76-78 would also be necessary.[16] Mr. Somnath Chatterjee also opposed the idea of a direct election of the President and stated that a stalemate would result if the President and the Prime Minister belonged to two different parties and this could lead to uncertainty and instability. Although, no concrete suggestion emerged from the panel discussion, Mr. Ghose concluded keeping in one tune with Mr. Snehanshu Kumar Acharjee that people of India would never indefinitely wait for the amelioration of their problems and hardship.[17]

It is very much relevant to note here that while inaugurating the Madabhushi Anantasayanam Institute of Public Affairs at Tirupati, Mr. R. Venkataraman, the former President of India remarked: "I feel that the subject is of relevance not only to India, but to all developing countries". He added, "in view of the Political instability, which has plagued our national Politics since 1989, and the danger of no one party being able to secure an absolute majority in the next or future elections, I have chosen for my address the theme, Stable national alternative to party government". According to him, it is true that the British Parliamentary practices appealed to most people in the world and was looked upon as an unerring model for others to follow. In India, however, during the first decade, when the stalwarts of the freedom movement brewed in selfless dedication, service and sacrifice held the command of the country, India functioned as a mature democracy and elicited the admiration of the entire world, including that of the sceptics who doubted the chances of adult franchise working satisfactorily among unlettered people. But thereafter, several weakness and flaws in the functioning of our democracy surfaced throughout the country costing considerably doubt over the stability and strength of the state and Central Governments. So as early in 1965, he submitted a resolution to the to the AICC asking for a Committee to examine and report, whether the present Cabinet form of Government at the Centre and the states may be replaced by an executive directly elected by the people for a fixed term of years, and if so, to recommended consequential changes in the constitution of India as appropriate. The resolution evoked the support of over 100 members of the AICC.[18]

The former President again, in 1991 in his address to the nation on the Republic Day stated that Parliamentary democracy in India has been going through a process of change. The phenomenon of one party enjoying a comfortable majority at the Centre has been replaced by a different configuration. He added, "In a multi-party Political System, we may not be able to avoid coalition government in the interest of the nation. Yet, there is a great deal of mental resistance to this concept, springing from the past familiarity with two-party system. It is time serious thought is directed towards the evolving pattern of our Polity".[19]

It has already been noted that the Draft Constitution in recommending the parliamentary system of executive has preferred more responsibility to more stability because of the fact that it has not been possible so far to devise a system which can ensure both in equal degree. But modern scholars believe that stability in any democratic system is an essential prerequisite for accountability. It is contended that there cannot be accountability unless there is stability. Hence, the two are complementary to each other. It is argued that the system of having a directly elected head of the state has certain obvious advantages as he will be more exposed to the people, more susceptible to public opinion and hence more accountable to the public.[20]

While agreeing the above view we have reasons to believe as Alan R. Ball (1993) points out that the Chief executives whether constitutional monarchs, civilian presidents or military dictators, are rarely representative in that they reflect the numerically dominant social class ethnic groups etc. in society. They are produced by by powerful groups such as the church or the army or they recruited by the political party machines. Armies supply the Chief executives in many developing political systems not only because of their monopoly of physical force but also from the concentration of technical and administrative competence in the armed forces and sometimes their ability to cut across tribal divisions.[21]

Mention may be made that in liberal democracies executives are recruited from the established political elites working through the political parties. Thus in Britain Labour Prime Ministers often have an almost identical social background to that of conservative Prime Ministers and Ramsay Mac Donald may be said to have been the only Prime Minister of working class origins.[22] Almost a similar position is found in India where a good percentage of the top political leadership continues to come from the top social strata.

It is important to note that the process of achieving the position is varied. As for example, in socialist regimes the emphasis is on the manoeuvring within the single party. Stalin achieved supreme power by his control of the party bureaucracy and his subsequent ruthlessness in dealing with party rivals.[23] Whereas in liberal democracies not only is the intra party battle usual but there is also the necessity of defeating rival political party leaders in competitive elections.[24]

As a matter of fact, the stability of the chief executive varies. Lord Bryce once remarked that "the problem" of constructing a stable executive in a democratic country in indeed so immensely difficult that anything short of failure deserves to be called a success".[25] This was Bryce's view of the office of the American President. The term of office of a president of the United States has only been interpreted by the death of the president, with one exception of Nixon's resignation, and further more the nomination for second term of office of an incumbent is seldom denied to him by his political party.

As regards parliamentary liberal democracies, the examples of France and Italy have been frequently quoted to illustrate the instability of the executive leadership, but Sweden and to a lesser extent Australia, show not only the long domination of government by one party but the stability of the government those parties have supported.[26] In Britain since 1945, Attlee in 1951 Home in 1964, Wilson in 1970, Heath in 1974 and Callaghan in 1979 have suffered reversals in general elections while holding the office of Prime Minister although conservative dominance after 1979 emphasises the stable elements in British cabinet government.[27]

It may be added that in British government the governing party's support for its leader and prime minister is very consistent. No labour Prime Minister has been forced out of office by his party. Similarly the conservative party, which has enjoyed office for longer periods, also reflects this basic stability of executive power. Only Balfour in 1905 Chamberlain in 1940 and Thatcher in 1990 can be said to have lost office through declining support in their own party. Balfour remained leader until 1911 and chamberlain resigned mainly as a result of the war and the need for a coalition. Both Eden in 1957 and Macmillan in 1963 resigned as a result of ill health, not specifically as a result of hostility in their own party. In the twentieth century only five ministers Balfour, Asquith, Lloyd George, Chamberlain, and Thatcher can be said to have been forced out of office through difficulties within the government party or parties, and only Mac Donald in 1924 and Callghan in 1979 have held general elections following parliamentary defeats.[28]

Alan Ball again rightly points out that it is a very difficult to discuss the stability of chief executive in liberal democratic systems without reference to the party system and the electoral system. Furthermore, the degree of stability of all these various governments is very similar when compared to the durability of chief executives in authoritarian regimes, e.g., Salazar, Mussolini and Hitler held power for thirty-six, twenty one twelve years respectively and Franco ruled for over thirty years.[29]

The Soviet Union on the other hand provided an illustration of stability and change in the socialist systems. Stalin died in 1953 after having monopolised all sources of executive power of the party and the state. His immediate successor Malenkov became both Chairman of the council of ministers and the equivalent of prime minister and the chief secretary of the central committee of the communist party, the most influential position inside the party. In the ensuing struggle for power with Khrushchev, Malencov relied on the state executive machinery as opposed to the control of party and his replacement as first secretary of the party in October 1953 by Khrushchev was followed in 1955 by Bulganin, Khrushchev's ally, replacing Malenkov as chairman of the council of Ministers. The seal was put on Khruschchev's victory by the expulsion of Malenkov and other opponents from the governing bodies of the party, the central committee and the presidium, in 1957. In 1958 Khrushchev replaced Bulganin as chairman of the council of ministers and appeared to have followed Stalin's example of concentrating party and state sources of executive power in his own hands. Khrushchev was successful in his leadership struggle because his political abilities and his career within communist party apparatus enabled him to secure support within the top levels of the party hierarchy.[30]

"Despite the example of Khrushchev", Ball points out, "the absence of a clear process of succession meant that it was very difficult to remove the leader consequently the tenure of leaders was very lengthy indeed. Only Poland saw frequent leadership changes partly because of factionalism within the communist party and partly because of assertiveness of its working class, whose protests were vital in the political upheavals in 1956, 1970, 1980-1 and 1988-98. In USSR Gorbachev tried to assure the institutionalisation of leadership in a new presidency, elected by parliament and subject to a maximum of two five-year terms of office. In the then Soviet Republics direct election of presidents, including Boris Yeltsin in Russia in June 1991, facilitated the transition from republic to independent statehood following the failed coup of August 1991.[31]

It is important to note in this context that the office of the chief executive whether Prime Minister, President etc. does invest the individuals concerned with authority that they do not posses as politicians and this strengthens their position against potential rivals. Moreover, the publicity and the opportunities to exploit the mass media are important factors. General de Gaulle was a master in the utilisation of television and his carefully staged press conference were designed to create the impression of aloof royalty unsullied by the real world of political bargaining and compromise with the political recruitment falling more and more into the hands of political parties, it is rare for a head of government to reach the top position without the ability and personality for political advancement. In fact, political parties in both socialist and liberal democratic systems provide thorough selection processes and the party is the key to exercise stability in these systems.[32]

In this context, mention may be made that party politics related to governmental stability in India is also closely related with caste identifications. Some political parties are explicitly organised to represent casts. Some others look primarily for caste-based support. Occupational interests also play a stronger part in states than in national politics, but since caste and occupation often overlap considerably, it is difficult to distinguish between caste and occupational conflicts.

As regards the pattern of party politics it may be noted that intense factionalism is present in almost all the political parties. There are many group conflicts within party organisations. It is rare that such conflicts are based exclusively, upon regional caste or other ethnic attachments and are indeed for such conflicts to be based exclusively upon class and occupational interests. While caste and religious conflicts tend to be intense, factional conflicts are fluid with more flexible relationships. The opportunities for skilful leadership capable of coalition building are therefore greater in a situation of factional politics than in a situation of conflicts based upon intense, primordial religious and cultural attachments. It fact these factors are responsible for the lack of institutionalisation of the party system and this along with increased competition at centre and state level cases instability as well as affecting the performance capacities of the government.

Another important issue related to the question of stability is the combination of federalism and the parliamentary form of government posed quite a few problems and challenges. For example, the basic philosophy of federalism generates decentralising tendencies, whereas the philosophy of parliamentary system reinforces centralising tendencies. Secondly federal systems are outcome of evaluation of the governance of the people in heterogenous, diverse and plural society inhabitating vast land tracts, while the parliamentary system is basically for governance of a homogenous people in a small country and thirdly the stresses and strains are likely between the Head of State and Head of Government, because the former is called upon to act in a dual capacity.[33] C.J. Friderich has proved with evidence that "it would seem that federalism ought from a practical point of view avoid the classic parliamentary system".[34]

So, in view of the reality of Political situation a new system capable of giving a stable government has to be devised. There is no doubt that Presidential system ensures stability of administration and at the same time provides continuity of polices during the currency of the term. In this pattern of polity the legislature and the executive derive their powers directly from the people. As a result, neither is superior or accountable to the other. The legislature may ensure the executive but it cannot curtail the term of executive or turn him out or office. The head of government will have a free hand in administering and resolving numbers complex problems that beset our country without making compromises for the sake of survival.

In 1970, another penal discussion on the theme "Has Parliamentary democracy failed in India" was organised by a New Delhi fortnightly, called "the State". Several well known personalities including B.K. Nehru, Charan Singh, K.M. Munshi, and R.Venkataraman were of the view that the presidential form of government offers the best solution to the problems created by the chaotic spectrum of splinter parties projected on the national scene in order to bring stability and progress. Such a proposal was again mooted by some prominent Congress members in 1975, but it did not gain currency. Mention may be made that in "Indian Democracy at the Cross-roads edited by S.A.H. Haqqi, the author has summed up as to why a constitutional expert like N.A. Palkhivala is of opinion that the Presidential system should be adopted: "First, it enables the President to form a cabinet consisting of competent, honest and outstanding men since his choice is not restricted to the membership of the legislature. Secondly, since the members of the cabinet are not the cleared representatives of the people. They have no interest in adopting cheap populist tactics. Thirdly, in the Presidential system the members of the government can concentrate on the job of governing the country instead of including in endless politicking. Fourthly, it would stop defections among legislators, which are mostly due to lure of office and Power.[35]

## References

1. The Statesman, 27th March, 2000.
2. *Ibid.*
3. *Ibid.*
4. *Ibid* 30 September, 2000.
5. Bakshi, P.M.: The Constitution of India Universal Law publishing Co. 1999 p. 88.
6. The statesman, 24th August, 1997.
7. Ghose, D.: *Ibid.*
8. *Ibid.*
9. *Ibid.*
10. The Statesman, 29 September, 2000.
11. *Ibid.* March 11, 1995 .
12. Dutta, Amal: India To-day, The Statesman, 11 July, 1997.
13. *Ibid.*
14. Ghose, D.: *Ibid.*
15. Bakshi, P. M.: The Constitution of India p. 61.

16. *Ibid* p. 149.
17. *Ibid.*
18. Speech by Mr. R. Venkataraman, the former President of India while inaugurating Madabhushi Ananta Sayanam Institute of Public Affairs at Tirupati, April 24, 1995.
19. *Ibid.*
20. R.K. Jaichandra Singh: The President System: An alternative pp. 115-118 quoted in Hansaria.
21. Alan R. Ball: Modern Politics and Government, fifteh edition: revised and updated, 1993 p. 171.
22. *Ibid.*
23. I. Deutscher: Stalin (1967) quoted in Alan R. Ball p. 172.
24. *Ibid.*
25. James Bryce: The American Commonwealth Vol. I, p. 72.
26. Alan R. Ball p. 173.
27. *Ibid.*
28. *Ibid.*
29. *Ibid.*
30. *Ibid.*
31. *Ibid.*
32. *Ibid.*
33. Hansaria, B. L.: Does India need a new Constitution? p. 9.
34. C. J. Friderich: Trends of Federalism in Theory and Practice p. 100 quoted in Hansaria p. 9.
35. *Ibid.*

# 7

# Which form of Presidential Government Would Suit Us?

In 1947, on the eve of India's independence, Winston Churchill said: "Power will go into the of rascals, rogues and free-booters. Not a bottle of water or a loaf of bread will escape taxation. Only the air will be free and the blood of these hungry millions will be on the head of Attlee. These are men of straw of whom no trace will be found after a few years. They will fight among themselves and India will be lost in political squbbles".[1] After more than four decades almost on the verge of the golden jubilee of India's independence Justice Krishna Iyer (1990) observed: "If the slide continues we may approach the stage of Government of, by and for the criminals".[2]

Yet, however, remote there is a silver lining in the fragile silhouette of good men that the Supreme Court in a bid to rid the system of criminals directed the election commission to ask candidates contesting parliamentary or assembly elections to mandatorily furnish details of their criminal antecedents, if any, to allow voters a chance to think before they make their choice.

"The little man may think over before making his choice of electing law-breakers as law-makers", said a three judge bench – comprising Mr. Justice M.B. Shah, Mr. Justice B.P. Singh and Mr. Justice H. K. Sema – while directing the election commission to pass necessary orders in this regard within the next two months.[3]

The order was issued by the Bench while disposing of an appeal filed by the centre challenging the sweeping directions of the Delhi

High Court on a petition filed by the Association for democratic reforms. Though the Supreme Court modified the High court order, it justified the same by saying that the High courts direction cannot be said to be "unjustified or beyond the jurisdiction".[4]

It is important to note that justifying the directions, Mr. Justice Shah said: "The adverse impact of lack of probity in public life leading to a high degree of corruption is manifold. Therefore, if the candidate is directed to declare his immovable and movable assets ... and that of his spouse and dependents it would have its effect". For example, the Bench continued if a candidate was required to disclose on affidavit assets held by him the voter can decide if he or she could be re-elected in cases where he/she is suspected to have made "tonnes of money" during his stint as a public servent.[5]

Hence it is a positive sign that the Supreme Court has begun a process that could transform Indian polity, provided that the Election Commission rises to the occasion, which includes not taking any nonsense from political parties. And if the Election Commission comes up with strict guidelines and enforcement norms on the five mandatory disclosures ordered by the court – a criminal conviction involvement in a criminal case, personal and family assets financial liabilities and educational qualifications – parties will have no option but to comply. If they pick shady candidates it will be in the knowledge that their past will become an easily accessible public record and, therefore, risk voter alienation. They will be under compulsion to pick clean candidates. It says something about Indian politics that most political parties will find the second choice difficult. It is really unthinkable about assembly elections without criminals. They will therefore, try to bypass the rules. That is where the election commission comes in.[6]

It is doubtful that how many criminal filthy rich loan defaulting and semi-literate politicians or those with only some of these qualities will come under the spotlight but it is hard to imagine a situation where political parties can get away with endlessly nominating candidates whose detailed curriculum vitae make them fit more for central jails than the central hall. Information is crucial element in choice, and the Supreme Court by holding that voters must know more has increased the possibility of better choices.[7]

Again the recent recommendation of the national commission

to review the working of the constitution assumes a bigger dimension with its final report submitted to the government. The commission has recommended reversing the procedure for forming the government. Instead of the Governor or the President identifying the largest party after elections and inviting its leader to form the government, the commission has recommended that a session of the assembly concerned or the Lok Sabha be convened to enable the legislators to elect their leader who would subsequently form the government. The leader's following in the House would be considered later.[8] Not only this, the commission is also reported to have recommended incorporating a provision in the constitution to limit the maximum period of preventive detention to six months with a view to protecting the rights of citizen. Incidentally, provisions of the Prevention of Terrorism Act (POTA) stipulate preventive detention of a period of one year. The panel has also explicitly suggested making freedom of the press a part of the fundamental rights of citizen.[9]

It is quite relevant to point out that the method of appointment of the head of the state executive by federal executive is repugnant to the strict federal system as it obtains in the USA and Australia. In actual working where one party has a clear majority, the part played by the Governor has been that of a constitutional and impartial head, but in those states where there are multiple parties with an uncertain command over the legislature, the Governor has acted as a mere agent of the centre in various matters such as inviting a person to form a ministry, because he belonged to the ruling party at the centre, even though he had no clear following (as in the case of Rajagopalachari in Madras, after the general election in 1952) or bringing about the removal of a ministry having the confidence of legislature, by means of a report under Art. 356 (as happened in Kerala in 1959, in the case of the Communist Ministry headed by Sri Namboodripad). Nevertheless, there is one aspect in which the system of appointing an outsider by the centre has proved to be beneficial and that is the prevention of disruptive and separatist forces from impairing the national unity and strength as might otherwise have been possible without the knowledge of the centre, under a locally elected Governor.[10]

A sharp controversy has arisen upon the question whether a Governor has the power to dismiss a council of Ministers, headed by the Chief Minister, on the ground that the Chief Minister and his cabinet have lost their majority in the popular House of the Legislature. According to Basu (1998) "the controversy has been particularly intriguing in as much as two Governors acted in contrary directions under similar circumstances. Mention may be made that in West Bengal, in 1967, Governor Dharma Vira, being of the view that the United Front Ministry, led by Ajoy Mukherjee had lost majority in the legislative assembly owing to defections from that party, asked the chief minister to call a meeting of the assembly at a short notice and on the latter refusal to do so dismissed the Chief Minister with his Ministry. On the other hand, in Uttar Pradesh in 1970, governor Gopala Reddy dismissed chief minister Charan Singh, on similar assumption, without even waiting for the verdict of the assembly which was scheduled to meet only a few days later"[11]. As a matter of fact, "the Governor of state has the power to dismiss a council of ministers only when the legislative assembly has expressed its want of confidence in the council of ministers, either by a direct vote of no-confidence or censure or by defeating an important measure or the like, and the Governor does not think fit to dissolve the assembly. The Governor cannot do so at his pleasure on his subjective estimate of strength of chief minister in the assembly at any point of time, because it is for the legislative assembly to enforce the collective responsibility of the council of ministers to itself, under art. 164 (2)".[12]

In its report to the centre the National Commission for review of the working of the constitution has called for several new fundamental rights including the right to expression, of which the right to freedom of press would form a part to be incorporated. The report has suggested bolstering provisions of article 14 of the constitution relating to equality before the law besides recommending the incorporation of several new fundamental rights. The commission has sought the inclusion of a right against torture and expansion of the scope of the rights to education[13].

There are far-reaching suggestions relating to electoral reforms, regarding which the Supreme Court in a bid to rid the system of criminals very recently directed the elected commission to ask candidates contesting parliamentary or assembly election to furnish compulsorily details of their criminal activities. Probably it will not be irrelevant to refer ignominy that the former chief election commissioner Mr. T.N. Seshan, who suffered a lot in trying to bring electoral probity which the amorality of politicians had defied. Mr. Seshan wanted to strike at the root of corruption in the country's electoral press and made attempts to free politics from the yoke of criminals.

It is unfortunate that so called national leaders started calling him "mad, bad and dangerous" and accused him of bolstering his ego as he stirred his constitutional authority to function. His courage and conviction in "not taking any nonsense from political parties" was taken as an affront to the dignity of our political bigshots. Political parties of almost all hues joined together to teach him a lesion. Parliament whose dignity and sanity was uppermost in Seshan's mind and whose degeneration he wanted to prevent by strictly enforcing electoral probity was used not to bring any censure against Seshan but to enact a law in order to clip his wings.[14] A mighty constitutional authority fell flat and was cut to pieces to facilitate its distribution among the pliable as far as possible.[15] In fact, what T.N. Seshan could not do has now started taking shape at the behest of the Supreme Court.

The present chapter would be incomplete without referring the Gujrat carnage. In the Lok Sabha on 30th April 2002 the treasury benches seemed to have a choice between two strategies when defending the conduct of the central and state government in the light of two-month ling carnage. When not blaming the victims they could, they could invoke the argument that there was nothing really new about it at all; the brutishness of the present could be explained by the mere fact that such behaviour had often been practised with impurity in the past[16]. Interestingly when a motion of a very similar in spirit but distinct in language came up before the Rajya Sabha the government benches chose a new track. Confronted with the reality that it would almost certainly be defeated in a vote the BJP-led National Democratic Alliance (NDA) moved alacrity to affirm its support for the motion. It soon woke up to the realisation that aversion to a symbolic defeat in the Rajya Sabha had pushed it into a position of virtually admitting to its delinquent ways. In its pursuit of debating points, the government was effectively rubbishing itself in public. And this was after a whole week of parliament's time had been lost in blocking the opposition's resolve to have a debate on the Gujarat situation. Again to the government's greater discredit, it had used the Lok Sabha as a platform to mount the less than inspiring spectacle of politicians venting partisan passion over the terrible human tragedy of Gujarat.[17] All those who witnessed the 17 hours of squabbling and sniping between the opposition and treasury benches in the Lok Sabha were left in a state of anguish over the depths to which the level of political debate had fallen. The government however won the vote in the Lok Sabha by a substantial margin. The motion which expressed concern at the handing of the situation in Gujarat secured only 182 votes whereas with 276 members voting against it and 8 members abstaining.[18] What has been evident from the debate on Gujarat in a two-faced government's dual track approach while some members were fielded by the NDA to ensure that the links with the politics of communual provocation are not lost Vajpayee and Advani with their measured seemingly well considered interventions sought to keep the restive allies on their side.[19]

It goes without saying that the recent unfortunate happenings specially in Gujrat, Assam and Kashmir have demonstrated that strong central control is needed in India if not only federalism but the very existence of the union of India is to be saved from separatist forces fighting for fragmentation which if undeterred would undermine that national unity integrity which forms the foundation stone of the constitution.

The most grievous feature of the post independence development in India is that the minorities have held up their vote as bait and political leaders of the majority community belonging to different parties including Marxist parties have indiscriminately swallowed that bait in their Election manifestos and alliances. To exploit the situation some leaders of the Muslim minority community is also now for a proportion representation in the legislatures and in the services according to their number.[20] This is in fact a resurrection of that baneful plant of the 'communal award' which had been inserted into the Indian body politic by British Prime Minister Ramsay Mac Donald and which had its inevitable culmination in the bloody partition of India and prevent any repetition of such anti national cleavages that the framers of the constitution of free India proclaimed the unity of the nation to be the objective in its preamble abolishing any reservation or representation on the basis of the religious colour of any individual or community and such reservation if made now would violate the guarantee of equality in Art. 15 (1) and 16 (1) –

(2), as explained by the Supreme court.[21] On this point it would be worthwhile to reproduce the illuminating words of Ahmadi J. who was in the nine judge case of Bommai v/s Union of India, (A. 1994 S.C. 1918) Ahmadi says: "The experience of partition of the contry and its aftermath had taught lessons which were too fresh to be forgotten by our constitution makers. It was perhaps for that reason that our founding fathers thought a strong centre was essential to ward off separatist tendencies and consolidate the unity and integrity of the country .... The British policy of divide and rule aggravated by separate electorates based on religion had added a new dimension of mixing religion with politics which had to be countered...". It was added since it was felt that separate electorates for minorities were responsible for communal and separatist tendencies, advisory committee resolved that the system of reservation for minorities excluding SC/ST should be done away with".[22]

Those who believe that communal harmony can be achieved only by granting more and more extra-constitutional privileges forget the adage – 'once an infant always an infant'. Experience goes that communal fascism is a vicious circle: the cry of 'Muslim in danger' gives birth Hindu fundamentalism and similarly the slogan of 'Muslim sentiments' has given rise to the plea of 'Hindu sentiments'.[23] There will be no end to these pernicious currents or cross currents so long as everybody is not convinced that all of us are bound by the constitution which we adopted as the 'people of India' under which there is no room for Hindu Indians or Muslim Indians, but there is only one nation, namely India which is solidly bound by a tie of fraternity.

India being inhabited by heterogeneous elements belonging to different races religions can maintain her independence only if she stands as one man inspired by a national sentiment. It is worthwhile to mention here that the country of America is also inhabited by heterogeneous elements but every American whether English, Hebrew, Italian or Negro origin regards the United States as his motherland for which he must fight against dangers at home or abroad and that is why she has maintained her independence as a mighty nation notwithstanding so much of difference in race religion and culture amongst her variegated population. The situation in India is just to the contrary. As in other matters, in India, even constitutional and legal questions are muddled up with politics, which of course means power politics. Most of the leaders of parochial political culture think little of the nation apart from the interests of the political parties to which they belong and through which machine they scramble their way to the seat of power. A structural change therefore, appears called for toward the guarantee of completion of a government's tenure with of course the legislature's power to reject a proposal or bill presented by the government. There is no doubt that this particular structure is provided for by the presidential system.

The American Government is considered a model of the Presidential system. The founding fathers of the American constitution were specially influenced by their own early constitutional experience of the absolute powers of the colonial Governors and the 'excesses of Democracy' during 1776 to 1787. Being guided by above experience they framed the American Constitution, which consequently gave institutional form to the theory of separation of powers. It is important to note that according to this theory individual liberty can be secured only if the three organs of the government are separated from one another. Keeping this in view, the framers of the constitution make clear the separate responsibilities of the three bodies. Thus, all the legislative Powers are vested in the Congress and these powers cannot be delegated to the executive. Again, the executive cannot issue ordinance, which have the effect of a Law, nor can it introduce bilis in the Congress. As regards executive powers, the President is the supreme authority. He implements the law, makes appointments with the approval of the Senate, runs the administration, conducts foreign Policy and commands the military forces of the country. The Supreme Court is the custodian of judicial powers. It resolves disputes and interprets the treaties and the constitution. Thus, the responsibilities of the three organs are clearly demarcated, neither superior to the other, the core Principle being that the executive is not accountable to the legislature for its activities nor does it control the legislature. This means the position of the American President is Secure in the sense that he enjoys a term of office fixed by the constitution and during this term, he cannot be removed from office either by the legislature or by the people except by the procedure of impeachment. Therefore, the US Government is considered a model of the Presidential form. Here, the legislative body, that is, the Congress is elected for a fixed term of two years for the House of Representatives and six years for the Senate by the people. The President is elected by the people for a fixed term of four years and the supreme Court judges, though appointed by the President with consent of the Senate, serve during good behaviour and are independent.

Following the example of the USA., third world countries including Latin America have adopted this form of government with variations to suit their conditions. And it is for the some of these reasons; General de Gulle of French revised its Constitution. Although, the Constitution of the France Fifth Republic, maintains the façade of responsibility of the executive to the legislature, it grants at the same time to the President such enormous powers that the Government resembles the Presidential rather than the Parliamentary form. Like the American system, the French President is also the choice of the people. He appoints the ministers and presides over their meetings and has wide emergency powers. He can dissolve the National Assembly.In fact; the President is the real head of the executive, master of the legislature and also of the Constitutional Council.[24]

It is however, important to note that although, theoretically presidential system requires clear demarcation of the legislative, executive and judicial functions each to be performed independently of the other but in practice, such strict separation has been found difficult to achieve and is found to be undesirable. Even in the U.S.A., devices are there for legislative and the executive functions to inform each other. Reference may be made in this context that the refusal by the Senate to ratify the Versailles Peace Treaties duly honoured by President Wilson is a proof positive of the real powers of the Senate.[25] R. Venkataraman 1965 observes – "The Presidential system obtaining in the United States where the Executive Head of the Country is elected directly to the office for a fixed term, offers stability of administration. The fact that the legislature is elected for a fixed term provides a measure of independence of thought and action to the legislators".[26] He also added, that 'the system has worked well in the United States. There are, of course, other variations of the system as the French constitution, which combines the Parliamentary fluidity with Presidential irremovability. There is no doubt, that Presidential system ensures stability of administration and provides continuity of policies during the currency of the term. It does not plunge the country into turmoil because of shifting loyalties of the members of the legislature, nor does it disrupt the term of the Executive because of the defeat of its proposals in the legislature.[27]

It therefore, appears to us that for reasons stated in the preceding chapters, the Presidential system of government may be adopted with some variations to suit India's condition for the sake of maintaining the unity and integrity of the Indian Nation. The question, however, remains, which model will be more relevant to the 'current coin' of our political discussion? Although, this is not the place for a detailed discussion of the comparative merits and defects of different models of Presidential form of Government, we can at least analyse some of the vital features of the systems which will lead us to conclude in support of our contention.

It is to be noted that the United status of America is not the only state having Presidential system of Government, there are a lot of other countries like France, Finland, Switzerland, Egypt, Sri Lanka and Philippines, Indonesia and Latin American countries like Argentina, Brazil, Chile, Costa Rica, Mexico, Uruguay, and Venezuela where this system prevails. South Africa is the latest such country.[28]

These countries have departed in many respects from the Presidential form adopted by America. Most significantly, France (since 1958) and Finland have mixtures of Presidential and Parliamentary institutions. The Presidents of both the States are directly elected by the voters independently of the legislature and serve for fixed terms. Both are Heads of state and also independently exercise a number of significant executive and legislative powers, including power to dissolve the legislature and hold new elections. As chief of state both Presidents are not only the symbolic and ceremonial heads of their nations but are also the principal makers and conductors of foreign policy. In addition, the French President can submit constitutional amendments for popular referendums without the consent of the Cabinet and the Parliament. In an emergency, he can suspend regular government procedures and take whatever measures he thinks fit.[29] In so far as Latin American democracies are concerned; the Presidential government are modelled on and remains similar to the United States system, though in some respects their Presidents are even more powerful. They have all the Powers of US President and have legislative veto Powers as well. Some Latin American countries can make all or most executive appointments without approval of the Legislature. Again, in respect of Presidential form in different countries of Asia, they have not adopted rigidly of the U.S. model but have conferred such powers on their Presidents, which were thought necessary for the ultimate good of the country.[30]

It shows that there is no fixed pattern of Presidential governments and each country has opted for such form and has bestowed such power on the President as was thought necessary as per the prevailing situation in the country. The point to be noted that the American President who is elected on an election manifesto outlining his policies may be thwarted by a Congress of a different political hue. As for instance the issue did arise in the United States when President Andrew Johnson was in office (1865-1869), in which a hostile legislature confronted a hostile executive and in which each may try to thwart and stultify the other.[31] On the other hand both the executive and the legislature have been so modelled in the French Constitution (The Fifth Republic) as to ensure the advantages of both British Parliamentary and American Presidential systems of government, at the same time avoiding their defects. Normally, powers are shared by both the President and the Premier but in times of a national crisis, the President Can assume all powers. Reference may be made of Article 16 of constitution which provides that in case of grave danger to the independence of the nation or the integrity of its territory when the regular functioning of the Constitutional machinery is interrupted, the President is empowered to take necessary measures to deal with the circumstances after official consultation with the Premier and the Presidents of the two assemblies as well as Constitutional council.

Again, we may refer here to the views of another eminent authority like Lord Bryce 1928 who has compared the merits of the English system of government with those of the American system. While dealing with the nature of the English system he says: "Its essence resides in the delicate equipoise it creates between the three powers, the ministry, the House of Commons and the people. The House is strong, because it can call the ministry to account for every act, and can, by refusing supplies, compel their resignation. The ministry are not defenceless because they can dissolve Parliament, and ask the people to judge between it and them. Parliament, when it displaces a ministry, does not strike at executive authority; it merely changes its agents. The ministry when they dissolve Parliament do not attack Parliament as an institution; they recognise the supremacy of the body in asking the country to change the individuals who compose it. Both the House of Commons and the ministry act and move in the full view of the people, who sit as arbiters, prepared to judge in any controversy that may arise. The House in touch with the people, because every member must watch the lights and shadows of sentiment which play over his own Constituency. The ministry are in touch with the people, because they are not only themselves representatives, but are heads of a great party, sensitive to its feelings, forced to weigh the effect of every act they do upon the confidence which their party places in them. The only conjuncture which this system of checks and balances does not provide for is that of a ministry supported by a Parliamentary majority pursuing a policy not presented to the people at the last general election, and of which the bulk of the people disapprove. This is a real danger, yet one which can seldom last long enough to work grave mischief, for the organs of public opinion are now so potent, and the opportunities for its expression so numerous, that the anger of a popular majority, perhaps even of a very strong minority is likely to alarm both the ministry and the Houses, and to arrest them in their course.[32]

In England, however, if the executive ministry displeases the House of Commons, the House passes an adverse vote. The ministry have their choice to resign or to dissolve Parliament. If they resign, a new ministry is appointed from the party which has proved itself strongest in the House of Commons; and co-operation being restored between the legislature and the executive, public business proceeds. If, on the other hand, the ministry dissolve Parliament, a new Parliament is set up which, if favourable to the existing cabinet, keeps them in office, if unfavourable, dismisses them forthwith. Accord is in either case restored. This method of cutting knots applies to all differences that can arise between executive and legislature. Whereas, in America a dispute between the President and congress may arise over an executive act or over a bill.[33] If over an executive act, an appointment or a treaty, one branch of Congress, the Senate, can check the President that is, can prevent him from doing what he wishes, but cannot make him do what they wish. If over a bill which the President has returned to Congress unsigned, the two Houses can, by a two-thirds majority, pass it over his veto and so end the quarrel; though the carrying out of the bill in its details must be left to him and his ministers, whose dislike of it may render them unwilling and therefore unsuitable agents. Should there not be a two thirds majority, the bill drops; and however important the question may be, and essential to the country some prompt dealing with it, either in the sense desired by the majority of Congress or in that preferred by the President, nothing can be done till the current term of congress expires. The matter is then remitted to the people.[34].

We may also refer here to the views of Professor Harold Laski 1938 who on this question observed that the Cabinet in England is essentially a committee of that party or coalition of parties, which can command a majority in the House of Commons. It is therefore, an instrument for linking the executive branch of Government to the legislative. It is the body, which directs the latter. The cabinet is an integral and living part of parliament and not separated from it. That the cabinet should be a committee of the legislature is one of the two or three main principles, which distinguish British System from that of the United States, and it is worthwhile to reflect for a moment on the consequences of the distinction. The essence of the difference between the two systems is that with the British System, the legislature has no interest separate from the executive whereas, in the United States, their separation gives it a separate interest. In England, therefore, the House of Commons must have confidence in as it were, its board of directors, otherwise there will be either a new board of directors or a new Parliament. But with the Americans, the Congress may have a different party complexion from that of the President and his cabinet colleagues; or he may have a majority in one House of Congress and not in another. Even with a majority in both, he need not have his way. He cannot control either House directly. He has no power to dissolve it. He can persuade, cajole, threaten, bribe but the life of the American legislature continues independently of his will. He sends his proposals but the Congress makes up its own mind what it will do with them. It is an authority of equal legal standing with him in the determination of policy.[35] In his contention, he added that the President of the United States is never the master of Congress except in relatively brief intervals of emergency. In fact, the House of Commons are only formally a legislative assembly. Its real business is to act as the cabinet's organ of registration. It may secure minor amendments, it may even, on rare occasions, secure the withdrawal of a proposal but fundamentally, legislation is shaped in Whitehall, and not in Westminster. With Congress, this is not the case. Legislation is the main business of both Houses. They do not act under the instructions of the President. They may co-operate with him if they feel so inclined. The analysis thus leads to the fact that whatever the weaknesses of the British system, it makes responsibility for action clear and direct and intelligible. An executive who cannot command the confidence of the legislature may appeal beyond it to the electorate. So long as it controls the legislature its authority is coherent and integrated. These are immense advantages. The authority may be abused, but at least, the responsibility for the abuse is always clearly indicated. The energy of the executive is not continually dissipated in patching up the majorities it requires for some degree of the programme it has urged. The allegiance of its supporters is not constantly shifting on its axis. There is not a constant interest in the legislature to develop a policy of its own at the cost of the executive credit.[36] In the United States, the only person responsibly charged with thinking and planning in terms of the whole union is the president, and it is a striking, even a startling, feature of the American scheme of government that he has no way of seeing that his conception of his duty will, as a normal feature of the political process, be weighed from the angle that he considers imperative.[37] Professor Laski reiterates that modern state requires disciplined leadership but the American system leaves no assurance of its continuous availability. It is, indeed, built upon foundations that are inherently suspicious of leadership as such. From the foundation of the Republic, the President has run in the leading strings of congressional control. This control has not presented a clear alternative to his leadership, rather, for the most part; its result has been a confusion of the public mind. He may move in one direction that is an invitation almost to congress to move in several other directions. The clash of opinion about the wisdom of the alternative he emphasizes does not lead back to the people from whom his authority emanates. According to him a democracy needs clear direction, and it cannot get this unless the central motive force in a political system rests in the executive's hands. He may be right or wrong: what is important is that the plans put into operation should essentially be plans for which he is willing to accept full responsibility. Secondly, it is not possible in the modern state to separate legislation from administration. In the making of policy, an assembly as miscellaneous as a legislature is bound to be, cannot organise itself for creative action unless those who direct organization are also those who will apply it in action. In the United States, this is not the case. There is always a separation, which at times may amount to an antithesis, between them. The system in fact, gives to the legislature functions, which nearly three-quarters of a century ago, John Stuart Mill pointed out it is least fitted to perform.[38] In referring to the question of separation of the executive from the legislature under the American Constitution, Prof Herman Finer 1950 observed: Congress makes the laws and Congress furnishes the funds. This is at once nourishes its corporate pride and its alienation from the executive. Each is invested with its own responsibilities; it is obliged to think of those first, always possibly above considerations of good government.[39] He also added that the American system of government is "enormously wasteful" as it severs executive knowledge from congressional lawmaking, and executive administration of the laws from the direct everyday impact of those who have made them and further, separates the making of policy from its fulfilment. This, he says, "is the normal predicament, even where a president and his party are well in the saddle in both Houses of congress. How much more so does this mutual stultification, but chiefly that of the President, weigh upon the nation, when, as too often happens, the party cannot simultaneously dominate legislature and executive. Each then steers a course towards a full victory over the other at the approaching elections: neither is willing to assist the other whole-heartedly though each may make pretence of this as an election tactic". As a result of the lack of confidence of the legislature in the executive incident to the American system of division of powers, hardly a day goes by without a threat by congressmen that they will not find the funds for the President's policies, especially for foreign policy and military expenditures, unless the President "tells us all the facts – all". But neither the House of Commons nor the French National Assembly is ever told all the facts nor can any assembly of hundreds of people, nor the people as a whole, ever be told all the facts, at the time they themselves demand.[40].

It is very significant to note that Woodrow Wilson, who was the President of the United States from 1913 to 1921, was not happy with the system of government prevalent there. About his own experience of the administration he stated: "Our federal executive and legislature have been shut off from co-operation and mutual confidence to an extent to which no other modern system furnishes a parallel. In all other modern governments the heads of the administrative departments are given the right to sit in the legislative body and to take part in its proceedings. The legislature and the executive are thus associated in such a way that the ministers of state can lead the houses without dictating to them, and the ministers themselves be controlled without being misunderstood, in such a way that the two parts of the government which should be most closely co-ordinated, the part namely, by which the laws are made and the part by which the laws are executed, may be kept in close harmony and intimate co-operation giving coherence to the action of the one and energy to the action of the other".[41] Of course, President Wilson is much more explicit in his criticism of the defects of the American system of government and in his appreciation of the merits of the English system. Indeed, according to Walter Lippmann, "he (President Wilson) would, if he could, replace the American Presidential system, which was according to him, radically defective, by the English System of Parliamentary government".[42]

Woodrow Wilson attributes what he considers to be the evils of he American System of Government to the separation of the federal executive from the federal legislature, the forcible and unnatural divorcement of legislation and administration and the consequent distraction of legislation from all attention to anything like an intelligent planning and superintendence of policy.[43] Regarding the inadequacy of legislative control over the executive departments of the American federal government and vice versa, Woodrow Wilson also remarked. "As for the executive departments, the people can hardly do more in drilling them to unquestioning obedience and docile efficiency than Congress can. Congress is, and must be, in these matters the nation's eyes and voice. If it cannot see what goes wrong and cannot get itself heeded when it commands, the nation likewise is both blind and dumb. This, plainly put, is the practical result of the piecing of authority, the cutting of it up into small bits, which is contrived in our constitutional system. Each branch of the government is fitted out with a small section of responsibility whose limited opportunities afford to the conscience of easy escapes. Every suspected culprit may shift the responsibility upon his fellows. Is Congress rated for corrupt or imperfect or foolish legislation? It may urge that it has to follow hastily its committee or do nothing at all but talk; how can it help it if a stupid committee leads its unawares into unjust or fatuous enterprises? Does administrative blunder and run itself into all sorts of straits? The Secretaries hasten to plead the unreasonable or unwise commands of Congress, and Congress falls to blaming the Secretaries. The Secretaries consider that the whole mischief might have been avoided if they had only been allowed to suggest the proper measures; and the men who framed the existing measures in their turn avow their despair of good government so long as they must entrust all their plans to the bungling incompetence of men who are appointed by and responsible to somebody else? How is the schoolmaster, the nation, to know which needs the whipping"?[44] It is impossible to deny that this division of authority and concealment of responsibility are calculated to subject the government to a very distressing paralysis in moments of emergency. There are few, if any, important steps that can be taken by any one branch of the government without the consent or co-operation of some other branch. Congress must act through the President and his cabinet; the President and his cabinet must wait upon the will of Congress. There is no one supreme, ultimate head whether magistrate or representative body which can decide at once and with conclusive authority what shall be done at those times when some decision there must be, and that immediately. Of course, this lack is of a sort to be felt at all times, in seasons of tranquil rounds of business as well as at moments of sharp crisis, but in times of sudden exigency it might prove fatal, either in breaking down the system or in failing to meet the emergency. Policy cannot be either prompt or straightforward when it must serve many masters. It must either equivocate, or hesitate or fail altogether. It may set out with clear purpose from congress but get waylaid or maimed by the executive.[45] It is to be kept in mind that Congress looks upon advice offered to it by anybody but its own members as gratuitous impertinence. At the same time it is quite evident that the means which congress has of controlling the executive departments and of exercising the searching oversight at which it aims are limited and defective. Its intercourse with the President is restricted to the executive messages, and its intercourse with the departments has no easier channels than private consultations between the executive officials and the congressional committees, informal interviews of the ministers with individual members of congress, and the written correspondence which the cabinet officers from time to time address the presiding officers of the two Houses of Congress, at stated intervals, or in response to formal resolutions of inquiry. Congress stands almost helplessly outside of the (executive) department. Even the special, irksome, ungracious investigations which it from time to time institutes in its spasmodic endeavours to dispel or confirm suspicious of malfeasance or of wanton corruption do not afford it more than a glimpse of the inside of a small province of federal administration. Hostile or designing officials can always hold it at arms length by dexterous evasions and concealments. It can violently disturb, but it cannot often fathom, the waters of the sea in which the bigger fish of the civil service swim and feed. Its dragnet stirs without executing the bottom, unless, it has at the head of the executive departments capable, fearless men, altogether in its confidence and entirely in sympathy with its designs, it is clearly helpless to do more than affright those officials whose conscience are their accusers.[46]

Woodrow Wilson concludes that the Federal Government lacks strength because its powers are divided, lacks promptness because its authorities are multiplied, and lacks wildness because its processes are round about, lacks efficiency because its responsibility is indistinct and its action without competent direction. It is a government in which every officer may talk about every officer's duty without having to render strict account for not doing his own, and in which the masters are held in check and offered contradiction by the servants. Talk is not sobered by any necessity imposed upon those who utter it to suit their actions to their words. There is no day of reckoning for words spoken. The speakers of a congressional majority may, without risk of incurring ridicule or discreet it, condemn what their own committees are doing, and the spokesmen of a minority may urge what contrary courses they please with a well-grounded assurance that what they say will be forgotten before they can be called upon to put it into practice, Nobody stands sponsor for the policy of the government.[47] "A dozen men originate it, a dozen compromises twist and alter it, a dozen offices whose names are scarcely known outside of Washington put it into execution. This is the defect to which it will be observed, I am constantly recurring, to which I recur again and again because every examination of the system, at whatsoever point begun, leads inevitably to it as to a central secret. It is the defect, which interprets all the rest, because it, is their common product. It is exemplified in the extraordinary fact that the utterances of the press have greater weight and are accorded greater credit, though the press speaks entirely without authority, than the utterances of Congress, though Congress processed all authority. The gossip of the street is listened to rather than the words of the law – makers. The editor directs public opinion, the Congress men obeys it".[48] Probably, there cannot be stronger condemnation of the American system of government than what Woodrow Wilson has thus made in his congressional Government.

Again, in his 'Government and Politics in the United states', Professor Harold Zink has stated, among other things: "The cabinet system goes far in guaranteeing harmonious relations between if there is lack of unity changes will be the executive and the legislative branches, if there is lack of unity changes will be made which will have the effect of restoring the equilibrium. Under this form of democratic government the two great executive and legislative branches must be geared closely together and except on rare occasions work toward the same end. Presidential government, on the other hand, is a contribution, which the United States has made to democratic institutions. Under a comparatively simple social system, the separation of the executive and the legislative branches are not provocative of acute problems. Since, relatively simple conditions existed in the United States during its early years; there was no crying need for integrating the two branches. As the industrial and social structures become more and more complex, the government was called upon to meet situations, which had never been envisioned by the forefathers. The lack of cohesiveness between the executive and the legislative departments became more and more evident, but the resourcefulness of the people made it possible to get along for many years without too great difficulty. The patronage system provided as extra legal tie of considerable strength; the political parties themselves contributed to a cementing of the executive and the legislative branches. Nevertheless, the system creaked and groaned under its burden of highly complicated problems, as an oxcart might if loaded with steel girders". Moreover, experience seems to prove rather conclusively that the traditional relationship between the President and Congress is not always satisfactory. Cabinet government provides far-reaching powers for the executive, but at the same time creates machinery for checking those powers when they seem to conflict with the national interest.[49]

Professors Frederic Ogg and Ormon Ray 1948 expressed the same view in their 'Introduction to American Government'. According to them under the Presidential form, there is much possibility of protracted discord division and frustration, with no assurance of relief until fixed terms of office expire and for this reason, as well as others, a good many people of the united states regard it as unfortunate that they started off with such a system and consider that, if it were at all practicable to win the necessary public approval, it would be desirable for them to go over to the cabinet plan, even at this late day. Professors Ogg and Ray, however, added that even under the American system, the national executive and national legislature, i.e., the President and Congress, are not in practice, completely isolated from each other but on the contrary they do actually maintain many close contacts and, by and large, become jointly the architects of most of their national legislation and public policy. Further, while there is not, and under the American constitution, cannot be, such an integration of authority as a cabinet system affords, the results attained need not always be, and some times are not, materially different.[50]

The above analytical observations amply justifies that there can be no successful government without leadership or without the intimate co-ordination of the organs of a Government.[51] It is also evident that a structural change appears called for toward the guarantee of Completion of a Government's tenure with of course, the legislative's power to reject a proposal or Bill presented by the Government. This particular structure is provided for by the Presidential system but due to innumerable weaknesses of the American presidential system, Mr. Venkataraman, the former President of India proposed a system which will replace confrontational politics by cooperative politics and a truly democratic alternative to the present constitution. His scheme does not envisage total scrapping of the Indian constitution which in his view is still good but not good enough to following stable national executive as an alternative to the Cabinet form of Government. According to him, there shall be a President to be elected in the same manner as at present or otherwise. The Prime Minister shall be elected as soon as may be after a general election or on the occurrence of a vacancy in that office by death, resignation or otherwise, by the Lok Sabha by means of the single transferable vote. The Prime Minister shall secure the support of more than 50 per cent of the members present and voting. The Prime Minister need not be member of either House of Parliament, but shall not continue in office unless he gets elected to either House of Parliament within six months of this assuming office. The same provision shall apply to members of the council of ministers.

The number of members of the Council of Ministers shall be fixed as 10 per cent of the strength of the Lok-Sabha. The number of members of the Council of Ministers from the Rajya Sabha shall be fixed at a percentage ranging from 25 to 33 or one third of the total strength of the Council of Ministers as may be decided at the time framing the new scheme. The Council of Ministers, however, shall be elected by means of single transferable vote by each House of Parliament as it is now being done in the case of Parliamentary committees.[52]

The Prime Minister and the Council of Ministers shall hold office for the term for Parliament and shall continue till the new Council of Ministers is appointed in the manner provided. Decision of the Council of Ministers shall be made by a majority of members present and voting. They shall not be removed by a vote of no confidence or on the failure of any of their proposals in Parliament. If vacancy arises in the Council of Ministers, it shall be filled in the manner in which vacancies in Parliamentary committees are being filled at present. The decision of Parliament shall be binding on the Council of Ministers. The Council of Ministers may, however, return for reconsideration of a part or whole of the measure and the decision of Parliament on such reconsideration shall be final and conclusive.[53] The validity of the Parliamentary decisions shall not be questioned except before the judicial authority competent to decide the same. It is also suggested that the ruling party members of the provisional parliament will recall that these members were free to criticise the Government, move amendments and even cut motions. Only they cannot vote against the Government as such a vote will entail the full of the Government. Since the defeat of a Government measure under the proposed Scheme will not cause the fall of the Government, the freedom to vote will cause no instability. As the Council of Ministers shall be elected by the whole House and not nominated by the ruling party, the anti-defection law becomes irrelevant.[54]

The former President also envisaged that the nation has to be protected against corruption and abused by the irremovable executive, viz., the Council of Ministers. It is therefore, necessary to provide for a constitutional authority at the centre to handle such cases. This authority shall have the same immunity as the judges of the Supreme Court. He suggested that constitutional authority might be named "Lok-Pal" and have jurisdiction over the Council of ministers, including the Prime minister and other elected functionaries of the government. A similar authority may be established to deal with the services. The states should likewise have a similar constitutional authority to deal with cases under this category.[55]

There is no doubt that the above unorthodox proposal deserves consideration in view of the political instability, which has severely damaged our national political culture. It is, however, difficult to implement because the proposal is based upon the presumption that "the decision of the Council of Ministers shall be made by a majority of members present and voting". It implies that complete co-operation of all political parties, is needed in the administration of the country, which is naturally impossible in India. This may be considered from an ideological point of view. The political culture always shows the trend, of sharp ideological differences between the Right and the Left. This will be evident from the fact that early in June, 1990 when Prime Minister V.P. Singh called for a National Government to overcome national crisis and offered to step down, all political parties including Rajiv Gandhi's Congress (I) and Jyoti Basu's CPI (M) took this in their various ways and rejected V.P. Singh's proposal.[56] Surprisingly, the different political parties were united by one short-term consideration, for immediate political gain. Whereas, there is such instance that during World War II, Britain's

National Government with Winston Churchill as Prime Minister had representation of conservative Labour and Liberal parties. It is important to note that Clement Attlee 1945-51 Prime Minister of Great Britain was also a minister in Churchill's National Government.[57]

The general consensus among the constitutional experts is that the success of a government depends on intimate coordination between the organs and as the French Presidential system combines the Parliamentary fluidity it is rightly believed that the French model is more relevant to India with Presidential irremovability it is rightly believed that the French model is more relevant to India. The French model maintains the facade of responsibility of the executive to the legislature but it grants to the President such enormous powers that the government resembles more the presidential than the Parliamentary form.

Let us now examine, how we may benefit by a study of the French Presidential system and why? In France, the president is elected for seven years by direct Universal suffrage (Art. 6-amended). The President is to see to the enforcement and working of the constitution. The maintenance of the independence of France and the integrity of its territory will be his first charge. According to Art. 5, "the President is the protector of the national independence, of territorial integrity and of respect for agreements within the community and for treaties".[58] He is to appoint the Premier on whose recommendation; he is to appoint other ministers. He can terminate their functions as well. Art. 8 of the new constitution says, "The President of the Republic shall appoint the Premier. He shall terminate the functions of the Premier when the latter presents the resignation of the government". Thus, it appears that the President nominates the Prime Minister – from among the members of Parliament or from outside similarly, the Prime Minister may nominate the members either from Parliament or outside but when a member of Parliament become a minister, he immediately resigns his seat in parliament and if an M.P. is nominated Prime Minister, by the President, he also resigns his seat in Parliament. Once a week the Prime Minister and his cabinet appear in Parliament to present their proposals and answers questions. The President, as the Executive head in the same way meets the Prime Minister and cabinet once a week and presides over the functions of the council of Ministers. It needs to be stated here that the ministry will be forced to resign if an absolute majority of members of the National Assembly pass a vote of no confidence. Art. 16 provides that in case of grave danger to the independence of the nation or the integrity of its territory when the regular functioning of the constitutional machinery is interrupted, the President is empowered to take necessary measures to deal with the circumstances after official consultation with premier and the Presidents of the two assemblies as well as the Constitutional Council.

A review of the powers of the President shows he is the real head of the executive and also co-ordinator of the legislature and as such the system provides for 'the fusion' of the executive power with the legislative power. Its essence, therefore, resides in the delicate equilibrium it creates between the executive and the legislature. We may also benefit by a study of French Presidential system, particularly in reference to the principle and practice of referendum, which if ever India adopts a Presidential system of government, should be anchor for polity's viability along with other safeguards against any latent desire of the rulers to have what Aldous Huxley refers to as 'uniform masses'. The referendum will protect our fundamental freedoms against the abuse of power. Of course, the obligation of holding the referendum needs to be guaranteed by the constitution.[59]

From the aforesaid background we have sufficient reasons to believe that Indian psyche and tradition have converted the Westminister system into a chamber for "horse trading" and "a game of numbers" stalemating the administrative and endangering public good.

Considering the increasing stability and weakness in the administration and considering the grave dangers of the territorial integrity of India caused by the growth of dissidents communalism and terrorism and especially from the threats of aggression from our neighbours, a structural change is the imperative need for stable governments both at the centre and states. In India, we may benefit by revising the constitution on the French model, which maintains the responsibility of the executive to the legislature and at the same time it grants to the president such powers that the government resembles the presidential rather than the parliamentary form. The system in words of Palkhivala will "enable the President to form a cabinet consisting of competent honest and outstanding men since his choice is not restricted to the membership of the legislature".[60]

## References

1. Ghose, D.: Presidential System: Only way pp. 1-2.
2. *Ibid.*
3. The Statesman, 3 May 2002.
4. *Ibid.*
5. *Ibid.*
6. *Ibid.*
7. *Ibid.*
8. *Ibid.*
9. *Ibid.*
10. Basu, D. D.: Introduction to the constitution of India pp. 225-226.
11. *Ibid.*
12. *Ibid.*
13. The Statesman 3 April 2002.
14. Bhattacharya, Khagen: Remember Seshan, The Statesman 12 May 2002.
15. *Ibid.*
16. Frontline: May 24 2002 P10.
17. *Ibid.*
18. *Ibid.*
19. *Ibid.*
20. All India Muslim Conference at Lucknow (The Statesman 29.12.1978); Muslim League's demand in Kerala (The Statesman 27.2.1983).
21. Basu, D. D.: Introduction to the constitution of India p. 407.
22. *Ibid.*
23. The Statesman 10.2.93 quoted in D. Basu's Introduction to the constitution of India.
24. Ogs and Zink: Modern Foreign Governments part-II pp. 24-27.
25. *Ibid.*
26. Speech given by Mr. Venkatraman, the former President of India while inaugurating the Madabhashi Ananta Sayanam Institute of Public Affairs at Tirupati 1995.

27. *Ibid.*
28. Hansaria, B. L.: Does India need a new constitution? p. 14.
29. *Ibid.*
30. *Ibid.*
31. *Ibid.*
32. *Ibid.*
33. Lord Bryce: The American Commonwealth, Vol. I 1928 pp. 288-290.
34. *Ibid.*
35. Harold Laski: Parliamentary Government in England; A commentary, 1938 pp. 220-225.
36. *Ibid.*
37. Ibid The American Democracy: A commentary and an Interpretation, 1949 pp. 75-77.
38. *Ibid.*
39. Herman Finer: The Theory and Practice of Modern Government, 1950 Ch. XXVI.
40. *Ibid.*
41. Woodrow Wilson: The State; Elements of Historical and Practical Politics 1919 pp. 377-378.
42. Banerjee, D. N.: Some Aspects of the Indian Constitution p. 32.
43. *Ibid.*
44. *Ibid.*
45. *Ibid.*
46. *Ibid.*
47. *Ibid.*
48. *Ibid.*
49. Harold Zink: Government and Politics in the United States, 1947 pp. 301-306.
50. Fredric Ogg and Orman Ray: Introduction to American Government, 1948 pp. 373-399.
51. W. Wilson: Constitutional Government in the United States p. 57.
52. R. Venkatramana: Speech given by the former President of India while inaugurating the the Madabhashi Ananta Sayanam Institute of Public Affairs at Tirupati 1995.
53. *Ibid.*
54. *Ibid.*

55. *Ibid.*
56. Ghose, D.: Presidential System only way, 1991.
57. *Ibid.*
58. Datta, A: India To-day; The Statesman, 12th July, 1999.
59. Ghose, D.: Presidential System only way, pp. 160-161.
60. S. A. H. Haqqi: Democracy at the cross-roads quoted in Hansaria p. 11.

# 8

# Conclusion

There is no doubt that the present structure and values of political system in India are largely the products of British colonialism. We can say that the British might have left India but for the average Indians the British colonial rule never ended in reality. Regulations drawn up by past colonial administrators are still being used, the draconian powers that the British used are still intact and are being used to stifle dissent. People are still being detained without trial, demonstrations are still harassed physically and newspapers are still shut down.[1] It is amusing to note that legal codes written by the British as far back as Queen Victoria's regime are still the law of the land – civil and criminal justice is dispensed on the basis of rules and regulations formulated by the British soon after the 'mutiny' of 1857.[2] In fact, all the features of a colonial system are present in our constitution. It has already been referred in previous chapters that India's present constitution is designed to recreate the 'colonial' parliamentary system instead of British parliamentary system. Dev Sharma 1998 rightly observes: The British always had two systems; one for themselves and the other for the colonies. Our constitution belongs to the latter category and contains all the features against which the American Revolution started in 1776.[3]

As a matter of fact, British Parliamentary system is not suitable for the soil of India because, the system which it pre-supposes is the existence of two great parties each strong enough to restrain the violence of the other and that where a third, perhaps a fourth party appears, the conditions are changed and consequently, the scales of Parliament oscillate as the weight of this detached group is thrown on one side or the other; dissolutions become more frequent and even dissolutions may fail to restore stability.[4]

As regards structural pattern and working of the political parties in India, it is everybody's experience that since independence from 1947 to 1967, there was one party dominant system the Indian National Congress with a tendency to bend parliamentary institutions to its needs only. It is surprising, observes Professor Mukherjee (2001) that Mrs Sonia Gandhi's reference to her family on the last day of 13th Lok Sabha session and the constant harping on the special status of the Nehru Gandhi family by senior Congress leaders is anachronistic in this age of democracy. This sort of disproportionate projection of a larger than life image calls for a serious dissection of the family's role in our democratic evolution.[5] He added that both Jawaharlal Nehru and Indira Gandhi personalised the political process. The very fact that a charismatic appeal is attributed to both of them means that they were far from the modern concept of a rational and legal authority.[6] It is evident from historical fact that any kind of charismatic authority is inherently unstable. Even the role that the Spanish King played in institutionalising liberal democracy in Spain after Franco's death had been greater than that of Jawharlal Nehru. Again Indira Gandhi's utter disregard for democratic norms and procedures was exemplified by the support she lent to V.V. Giri against Sanjeeva Reddy, the officially chosen Congress candidate for the presidency.[7] Other examples are her disregard for the Allahabad High Court judgement, imposition of internal emergency and subsequent amendments to the constitution to safeguard her interests.

Mention may be made that in 1977 and 1979 frequent defections from one party to another had reduced parliamentary democracy to a farce. The proliferation of political parties has now reached a saturation point leading to an all – pervasive and growing apprehension of political instability inflicting serious implications on our socio – economic life. Westminster system turned out to be abetting the destabilisation process and defections. Mr. V.P. Singh in his closing days as Prime Minister coined this system as "game of numbers" and Mr. Madhu Dandavate, the Finance Minister termed it as "horse-trading". This is extremely bizarre and disturbing and there is nothing to stop businessman from wooing legislators in groups. They have the money and in this game of numbers considerable unaccounted money is deployed[8].

Recently, the tehelka.com revelations and their aftermath shake up entrenched political – bureaucratic networks and conduits in New Delhi that seek to milk the governmental system to their advantage.[9] The incident shows how the democratic credentials and leadership can easily be purchased through the illicit take from the dispensation of patronage. More chastening has been the realisation that it is quite so simple for two rank amateurs making up in audacity for their ignorance of defence matters to enter the portals of the country's most highly secured establishment and work their way up through judiciously placed pecuniary favours.[10]

A more striking event is the trend, which revealed since the General Election of 1980 regarding the ever-aggressive demands of the religious minorities. The most grievous feature of this post – independence development is that the minorities have held up their vote as bait and political leaders of the majority community belonging to different parties have indiscriminately swallowed that bait in their election manifestos. The major demand of Muslim minority community now is for a proportional representation in the Legislatures and in the services according to their number.[11] This is nothing but a resurrection of that baneful plant of the 'communal award' which had been inserted into the Indian body politic by British Prime minister Ramsay Mac Donald ultimately culminated in the bloody partition of India.

It will not be irrelevant to point out here that the framers of the constitution of India deliberately proclaimed the unity of the Nation to be objective in its preamble, abolishing any reservation or representation on the basis of the religious colour of any individual or community only to prevent any repetition of such antinational cleavages. It is very significant to note that such reservation, if made now, would violate the guarantee of equality in Arts. 15 (1) and 16 (1) (2) as explained by the Supreme Court.[12] Of course, all these guarantees acknowledge the constitutionality of reservation or other special provisions in the interests of the 'backward classes', so that any community which is socially or educationally backward may be entitled to special consideration under the existing constitution Art. 15 (4), irrespective of its religious complexion. But strangely enough, they demand reservation for a man because he is a Muslim or a Christian even if he be affluent! It is to be kept in mind that to make any special provision for such a person would be a discrimination against the majority violating the rights of equality guaranteed by Arts. 15-16.

It is alarming that to accept such anti-nationalist demands of the minority would mean to tear India into pieces with a second Pakistan for Muslim majority areas or a Christendom for the Christians or an Islamic Republic for the Muslims or a Khalistan, so far as the Shiks are concerned or a Buddhist Republic so far as the Buddhists are concerned and so on.[13] In support of this statement Basu 1998 observed "the meek demands are crystallised and further extended, taking advantage of the fact that non-Muslim political parties vie with each other in conceding such demands, in whole or in part, in order to secure Muslim votes".[14] It is unfortunate that the manifestos of Congress (I) and the Janata Dal for the 1991 election promised reservations for the minorities in the government service and the armed forces. This was how Pakistan was built up. The same history is being repeated. Thus, while originally the demand was for communal representation in the government services, the Indian Muslim League has since 1979 extended the demand to such representation in the public sector undertakings and technical establishments, the army and the police. Similarly, the demand for aid for the promotion of Urdu has come to be a demand that Urdu should be recognised as an official language under Art. 347 of constitution even in those states where the Urdu speaking people do not form a substantial proportion of the population of the state concerned, such as West Bengal. The paradox of the situation is that while in Bangladesh, the Muslims themselves are fighting for the propagation of the Bengali language, the Muslims of West Bengal whose mother tongue is Bengali are making a frantic effort to speak in Urdu and also to represent at the time of census that their mother tongue is Urdu.[15]

The dangerous anti-national trends are also evident from the fact that during United Front Ministry in Kerala 1967-69, a separate Muslim district was formed, named Malapuram and surprisingly in 1983, the United Democratic Front government, led by Congress (I) has conceded the demand for the formation of a second Muslim majority district with Kasargad as its headquarter.[16] Again, Jamiat-Ulma-i-Hind goes to the extent of urging for the deletion of Art. 44 which mean a uniform civil code throughout the territory of India should not be applicable to the Muslims who should be allowed to be governed by the 'Shariyat' as their personal law. This type of demand was however, not unknown at the time of framing of the constitution but such demand was rejected on the ground that, matters like marriage, inheritance and the like falling under the category of 'personal law' are secular matters having no essential relation to religion. Secondly, without a common civil code, inter alias, the people of India, belonging to heterogeneous elements, could never be united into a nation. This provision in Art. 44 is nothing but an implementation of the objective of 'fraternity unity and integrity of the nation' which is not only enshrined in the preamble to the constitution, but is since buttressed by the fundamental duties in Art. 51A (C).[17] Surprisingly, the government of India in 1986 undertook legislation to supersede the law declared by Supreme Curt in Shah Bano's case deprived the Muslim women of the rights that they enjoined in common with all other women.[18] It is very much unfortunate that the Congress (I) government just for the sake of vote-catching motive gave way to the Muslim fundamentalists to violate the Supreme Court decisions as well as the constitution which enjoined the state to make a common civil code, overriding any personal law to the country. It is also very surprising that even the National Front government dittoed that and declared there would be no civil code unless the Muslim Community wanted it.[19] Quite helplessly the Supreme Court observed in the judgement of Ahmed V. Shah Banu case 1985: it was a pity that the state had not made any attempt to make a common civil code even though Art. 44 issued a clear mandate on the state.[20]

A more fundamental cause of the trend towards the failure of Parliamentary democracy is probably the controversy regarding the appointment of Miss Jayalalitha as chief minister who was convicted of corruption and disqualification for membership of the legislative Assembly.[21] It is being argued unabashedly without any moral or legal compunctions that under Art. 164 (1) that the Governor has an unfettered right to appoint anyone as the chief minister as if while there are qualifications and disqualifications for being 'members', there are none for being 'ministers'. Art. 164 (4) is being interpreted to mean that even disqualifications for membership do not apply to occupying ministerial office for six months. This argument is not tenable because Art. 173 of the constitution lay down the minimum qualifications for membership of houses of state legislature in terms of age and citizenship and says that additional qualifications may be prescribed by parliament by law. Art. 191(1) lays down the disqualifications. These are: (i) Holders of office of profit under the government, persons of unsound mind so declared by court, persons who are undischarged insolvents, (ii) Those who are not citizens of India, (iii) Those who are disqualified by or under a law made by parliament. Section 8 (3) of the Representation of the People Act 1951, specially provides that a person convicted of an offence and sentenced to imprisonment for not less than two years shall be disqualified from the date of such conviction and for six years after release.[22]

The foundational principle of the parliamentary system is that the executive comes out of the legislature, remains part of it and is always responsible to the popular House, Members of the Council of Ministers, therefore, have got to be from among the members of the legislature. The basic principle requires the ministers to be members of the legislature clearly suggests that only those eligible or qualified to be members can be appointed as ministers or chief ministers. Anyone who stands disqualified from being a member stands doubly disqualified from being appointed a minister or chief minister so long as the disqualification lasts.[23]

So, if a disqualified person can be appointed and can continue as a Chief Minister for six months, then not only those convicted of some of the most heinous offences but even those who are not citizens of India, are bellow 25 years of age, are occupants of offices of profit under the government, or are insane or insolvent would become eligible for Chief Ministership. That certainly could never be the parliamentary practice anywhere in the world and certainly that could never be the intent of the founding interpretation. What the Tamilnadu Governor did on 14th May 2001 was nothing but a sheer surrender to blackmail. Sam Rajappa 2001 rightly noted: If only Prime Minister Atal Behari Vajpayee respected the unanimously passed resolution of State unit of Bharatiya Janata Party to recall Tamilnadu governor Fathima Beevi, and a similar resolution by DMK, leader of National Democratic Alliance in the State, for showing scant regard to the spirit of the constitution and democratic norms in inviting Jayalalitha of AIADMK— a criminal convicted thrice over and sentenced to varying jail terms but on bail granted by Madras High Court— to form the government, the nation could have been spared the ignominy of having in the Indian Union a, banana republic where jungle raj prevails.

It appears especially from the beginning of the present decade that violence and extermination of opponents is being restored to as an easier mode of winding an election. It is a common feature that even a chief minister does not hesitate to declare openly the result of a poll because the issue of a certificate of the returning officer is under his control. Another chief minister who is convicted again and again wanted to dust the twenty-five years old Sarkaria Commission report which was itself a part of emergency excess of Indira Gandhi and the CBI had failed to establish any of the charges contained therein in a court of law. It was given a quiet burial.

It is apprehended that if this trend is allowed to continue and if conscious citizens do not cry a halt to him criminalisation of politics there will be total death knell of parliamentary democracy in India. Justice Krishna Iyer 1990 aptly remarked, "If the slide continues, we may approach the stage of Government of, by and for the criminals".[24]

Considering the increasing instability, dangerous anti-national trends, criminalisation of Politics, Corruption and weakness in the administration caused by the growth of dissidents and groupism in the country, the need for Presidential form of government was felt by no less a person than Shri R. Venkatraman, the former President of India. As a member of the Planning Commission he had given a notice as early as in May, 1965 to move a resolution in the session of AICC for seeking to change the constitution by having directly elected executive both in the centre and states. Five years later, when a New Delhi fortnightly, called, 'The State' set the theme, 'Has Parliamentary democracy failed in India?' and invited discussion several well known personalities including B.K. Nehru, Charan Singh, K.M. Munsi and R. Venkatraman were of the view that the Presidental form of government offers the best to the crisis caused by the chaotic spectrum of splinter parties.[25]

Subsequently, renowned constitutional expert Shri N.A. Palkhivala argued that presidential form of government enables the directly elected executive to form a cabinet consisting of competent, honest and outstanding men since his choice is not restricted to the membership of the legislature. Not only that, since the members of the cabinet are not elected representatives of the people they have no interest in adopting cheap populist tactics. He added that, in the presidential system, the members of the government can concentrate on their job of governing the country instead of indulging in endless politicking. Finally, Shri Palkhivala opines that the system would stop defections among legislators which are mostly due to lure of office and power.[26]

In 1984, the Press club of Calcutta organised a panel discussion on "will the Presidential system of government help India?" The participants were Mr. Ashoke Sen, Mr. Basant Sathe, Mr. Justice Krishna Iyer, Mr. S.K. Acharya, Mr. Bhola Sen and Mr. Somnath Chaterjee. Mr. Dipankar Ghose, the renowned journalist acted as the moderator who placed on record the stand of Mr. Sathe and other leaders endorsing his views that the public purpose would be best served if a system could be evolved that would ensure two aspects of government. As for example, the power of the legislature is to reject the executive's proposals and the right of the executive to continue in office for its full term despite losing the legislatives support as in the USA or France.[27]

Mr. Hansaria (1998), former Judge of the Supreme Court of India observed, "in the present political scenario, which has continued for quite sometime and is likely to so subsist in near future, the presidential form has become the need of the hour, as in the present system many hic-cups have appeared and the executive government has failed to take bold decisions, otherwise required for betterment of the people to remain in power. The result has been the poor remaining the poor. A presidential form of government, with real executive power in the President and security of his tenure for a fixed period will take care of the 'saving of skin' aspect and the President will be able to take required steps without fear of losing his 'gaddi'.[28] It may be noted in this context that even in parliamentary form of government sometimes a prominent leader of political party contesting election is projected as future Prime Minister, in case that party were to form government after the election. In England, however, this has become a common feature. Now, if that very person becomes the President in the other form of government, the possibility of his becoming a turncoat and working at his whim has to be ruled out; at least not to be given such as to outweigh the advantages of the presidential form. Further, to take care of this apprehension, provision may be made in the constitution that matters of great public interest, like the declaration of war and imposition of emergency, would need Parliament's ratification without specified time failing which such actions will become non-operative. To put it differently, the constitution may provide for some check on the power of the President to see that he does not become an autocrat.

It is evident from the above observations that the presidential model will effectively plug some of the inherent weakness of our present Parliamentary system, responsible for electoral corruption, defection, mid-term polls and coalitional bargaining. The Supreme executive head, that is, the President can offer executive posts to men of talent and exceptional merits and need not limit his choice to politicians only. Besides, stability will not be impeded because there will be no reason for political defections. The undivided executive power would get concentrated and generate quick decisions.

Of course, question is generally raised that this sort of undivided executive power will tend towards centralism and centralisation will impair federal reflections and imperil civil liberties. It is, however, important to note that the combination of federalism and the parliamentary form of government always poses problems and challenges. For example, the basic philosophy of federalism generates decentralising tendencies, whereas the philosophy of parliamentary system reinforces centralising tendencies. Again, federal systems are outcome of evaluation of the governance of the people in heterogeneous diverse and plural society inhabiting vast land tracts, while the parliamentary system is basically for the governance of a homogeneous people in a small country.[29] Hence, from practical point of view India should avoid the classic parliamentary system.

The aforesaid shows the shortcomings and defects inherent in our system of governance. The political practices should rise above narrow party politics and come to terms with reality and make an in-depth study whether improvement of the existing system with adjustments and modifications will do or whether we need a complete switchover to any other model.

It is important to note that the founding fathers did not have the vision not to rule out revision or improvements of the constitution, which was never intended to be static, nor does it claim to be infallible. Dr. Ambedkar himself said: "This constituent Assembly has not only refrained from putting a seal of finality and infallibility upon the constitution by denying the people the right to amend the constitution...... but has provided the most facile procedure".[30] It is unfortunate that in the 50th year of independence, when government proposed to set up a constitution review committee to go into the question of comprehensive examination of the constitution and suggest changes, if any to realise the goals set in its preamble. Some political parties out of political motivation unnecessarily raised hue and cry. They contended that the move to bring in one – party dominant system in the country through the presidential form to be sinister. This is however, improper to air opinions even before the committee is formally constituted.

As regards modality to be adopted, if new constitution is favoured, people's views shall be required because the constitution to be framed would be for the people of India. For this purpose, a referendum on the question is deemed necessary. Mention may be made in this context, that referendum process has been widely used in many democratic countries like United States, Switzerland, Australia, New Zeland, France, and Scandinavia and to a lesser extent in Ireland and United Kingdom.[31]

It should be borne in mind that constitutional reform is the most important field for referendum. After a national upheaval, a country may seek legitimating for the new regime and the rules under which it is to be run as occurred in France in 1945-1946 after World War II and in Spain in 1977 in the transition after General Francisco Franco's regime. It may be noted that the major constitutional matters to the people; for example, the form of the electoral system (New Zealand in 1992 and 1993. Italy 1993), the power of the Senate (France, 1959); the status of monarchy (Belgium, 1950; Greece, 1974); or voting age Denmark, 1978).[32]

Benjamin says, "In the United States, the submission to a vote by the representative body, came to be introduced in three different forms at three different periods of American history. The device of the modern referendum first appeared in the United States in the form of submitting state constitutions to the people for rectification, and this was tested in Massachusetts in 1778. In later years, especially after 1820 almost all-new state constitution was submitted to the popular vote. The practice was not confined to the adoption of a state coalition, but was also extended to what the Swiss called the partial revision of a constitution; this subsequently came to be known as the constitutional referendum, the purpose which was to refer a constitutional issue to the whole electorate. The essence of the referendum, therefore, was that it submitted a question to the general body of citizens, and it became 'the most direct and democratic method' of consulting the public..... In the United Kingdom, the device was used largely for local governmental issues and the Public Libraries Act of 1850 provided for local authorities to hold referenda among ratepayers before establishing public libraries. The constitution of the Fifth Republic of France provided for referenda only on bills and five referenda have been held; one, in fact, was held on the constitution itself".[33].

Now, in the above background if referendum takes place in our country, it may require the electorate to indicate their choice of the candidates who shall come forward to become members of the new constituent Assembly. This choice, of course, would be exercised by those who would desire framing of a new constitution. For those who would not, the question of choosing proper members for the new constituent Assembly would not arise.

The positive aspect of this type of referendum-cum-election would obviate the need of approaching the people twice – once to know whether they desire a new constitution and if the majority were to answer the question in affirmative, then to ask them to elect members for the new constituent Assembly. This procedure would avoid spending of money, time and energy twice over, it would also avoid straining the resources of the country too much.[34] It is however, apparent, that the election part would become only relevant if the main question regarding the need of new affirmative by the majority.

From the aforesaid contention if majority people desire to switch over to presidential type from the present Victorian model to overcome constitutional crisis, the relevant question necessarily follows which form of presidential government can set the wrongs rights? The American model can not be suitable for India on the ground that in combining stability with responsibility, they gave more importance to the latter and preferred the system of 'daily assessment of responsibility' to the theory of periodic assessment upon which the American system is founded.[35] Again, under the American system conflicts are bound to occur between the executive, legislative and judiciary and on the other hand, according to many American scholars, the absence of co-ordination between the legislatures and the executive is a source of weakness of the American political system. It may be noted in this context that the present author while staying in the University of Arizona, USA as a visiting scholar proffered a seminar on the "Institution of American presidency and its relevance to India" a number of University Professors including Dr. Zim Clarke, the Head of the Department of Political Science, Arizona University had objected American model because such model engenders the political climate of authoritarianism emanating from manipulated public opinion and sustained by stage managed public accountability. Almost all the teachers and research scholars favoured the French model as the ideal type of government, which maintains a smooth coordination between the legislature and the executive.

It may be stated that countries like France since 1958 and Finland have mixtures (see Appendix II & III) of presidential and parliamentary institutions. The Presidents of both countries are directly elected by the voters independently of the legislature and serve for fixed terms. Both are heads of the state and also independently exercise a number of significant executive and legislative powers, including power to dissolve the legislature and hold new elections.[36] As chief of state both Presidents are not only the symbolic and ceremonial heads of their nations but are also the principal makers and conductors of foreign policy. In addition, the French President can submit constitutional amendments for popular referendums without the consent of the cabinet and parliament. In an emergency, he can suspend regular government procedures and take whatever measures he thinks fit.[37] It needs to be stated here that France's President nominates the Prime Minister from among the members of parliament or from outside the parliament and the Prime Minister nominating the Ministers, either from Parliament or outside. If a Member of Parliament becomes a Minister, he immediately resigns his seat in Parliament. If an M.P. is nominated Prime Minister by the President, he also resigns his seat in Parliament.

In India, we may benefit by this reference to the principle and practice of referendum, which is in spirit close to the declaration of human rights. The positive aspects of such system are both innovative, realistic and suited to the problems created by the chaotic spectrum on the national scene in order to bring stability and progress.

As a matter of fact, the proposed review of the constitution is an opportunity to consider the historical circumstances, which was responsible for framing the political context in which the Indian constitution was written. We must not forget that western political institutions and conventions were introduced under colonial rule. They operated within the framework of an arbitrary and authoritarian regime, rather than an open democratic regime. As a result, the present constitution does not provide people with real power except to vote. The people in fact are used to cast their votes and then they are discarded.

The impact of colonial rule, therefore, impeded the groundwork for democracy in India as happened during the evolution of democratic and parliamentary institutions in the United Kingdom from the sixteenth century onwards. Constitutional codes had to function in India, thus, in something close to an ideological vacuum through fragile institutions.[38] This became obvious as stated in chapter IV 'crisis in Indian politics' instability in the political arena, unlawful activities like capturing booths during elections, bloodshed, horse-trading, dangerous antinational trends and above all, weakness in the administration caused by the growth of dissidents and groupism in the legislative party amply demonstrate not only inherent deficiencies of the parliamentary form of democracy but sound its 'death-knell'.[39] In the circumstances "thoughts" as Ghose (1991) remarks, "cannot but turn to the long mooted proposal of the present Westminster Model's replacement by the presidential system ensuring: installation of a stronger and more effective executive against economic offenders, committed to act independently of economic interest groups and without fear or favour, complete its fixed period of tenure unaffected by the loss of legislature support and only at the end of the fixed period, accountability to the voter".[40] But in this context, a jurist should obviously point out that this will not be possible because of an amendment of the constitution, which will not be tolerated by the Supreme Court so long as the 'thirteen – judge' dogma that the parliamentary system of government is a 'basic feature' of our constitution is not turned down by a larger bench.[41]

A new constitution for this purpose is indeed a desideratum and in this respect, the framers of the constitution should rise above party politics and affiliations. Their consideration should be national interest only. It is also relevant to probe if the French experience on the use of the referendum could ever help India.

As regards the basic question on the 'thirteen judge' bench decision dogma regarding changes in the basic structure that is, adoption of Presidential form in place of Parliamentary the concluding answer probably will be, "constitution is after all meant for the people and if they be of the view that the one at hand has failed to deliver goods, they have the undoubted right to give them another constitution.[42] There is no legal impediment, no moral prohibition. Let the people who gave unto themselves this constitution decide this vital question.

## References

1. Dev Sharma, Keshav: What constitute India? The Statesman 24th May, 1998.
2. *Ibid.*
3. Lord Bryce: The American Commonwealth, Vol. I 1928 p. 88.
4. Mukherjee, S.: Let Histry Judge, The Statesman June 9, 2001.
5. *Ibid*, June 28, 2001.
6. *Ibid.*
7. Ghose, D.: Presidential system only way, 1991 p. 4.
8. Frontline April 13, 2001.
9. *Ibid.*
10. *Ibid.*
11. *Ibid.*
12. All India Muslim conference at Lucknow Statesman 29th December, 1978; Muslim Leagues' demand in Kerala Statesman 27th February, 1983.
13. Basu, D.: Introduction to the constitution of India 18th Edition, 1998, p. 408.
14. *Ibid.*
15. *Ibid.*
16. Ananda Bazar Patrika, 28th August, 1985 quoted in D. Basu's Introduction to the Council of India, 1998.
17. The Statesman, 27th February, 1983.
18. Basu, D. p. 409
19. *Ibid.*
20. Ibid

21. Hansaria,: Does India need a new constitution p. 10.
22. *Ibid.*
23. *Ibid.*
24. Basu, D.: Introduction to the Constitution of India p. 409.
25. Hansaria,: Does India need a new constitution p. 10.
26. *Ibid.*
27. *Ibid.*
28. Ghose, D. pp. 148-149.
29. Hansaria, B. L. p. 13.
30. Sharma, R.: The Federalism, Presiding and Parliamentary system, p. 256.
31. Nadi, M.: Good Government, The Statesman 30 March, 2000.
32. Hansaria p. 66.
33. *Ibid.*
34. Hansaria,: Does India need a new constitution? Quoted from Recent Politics in Srilanka by W. A.Wiswa Warapala and L. Dias Hewagaura, 1983 pp. 126-127.
35. Hansaria pp. 63-65.
36. Basu: Introduction to the Constitution of India p. 188.
37. Hansaia p. 15.
38. Sems: Political Culture The Statesman 17 Feb, 2000.
39. Ghose, D. p. 19.
40. Basu, D. p. 419 case ref.
41. Hansaria p. 66.
42. *Ibid.*

# Appendix I

# Relevant Part from the Constitution of United States of America (1787)

Article II

**Section 1.** (1) The Executive power shall be vested in the President of the United States of America. He shall hold his office during the term of four years, and, together with the Vice-President, chosen for the same term be elected as follows:

(2) Each State shall appoint in such manner as the Legislature thereof may direct, a number of electors, equal to the whole number of Senators and Representatives to which the State may be entitled in the Congress; but no Senator or Representative or person holding an office of trust or profit under the United States, shall be appointed an elector.

(3) The electors shall meet in their respective States, and vote by ballot for two persons, whom one at least shall not be an inhabitant of the same State with himself or herself. And they shall make a list of all the persons voted for, and of the number of votes for each; which list they shall sign and certify and transmit sealed to the seat of the Government of United States, directed to the President of the Senate. The President of the Senate shall, in the presence of the Senate and House of Representatives, open all the certificates, and the votes shall then be counted. The person having the greatest number of votes shall be President, if such number be a majority of the whole number of electors appointed; and if there be more than one who have such majority, and have an equal number of votes, then the House of Representatives shall immediately choose by ballot one of them for President; and if no person have majority, then

from the five highest on the list the said House shall in like manner choose the President.

But in choosing the President, the vote shall be taken by States, the representation from each State having one vote; a quorum, for this purpose, shall consist of a member of members from two-thirds of the States, and a majority of all the States shall be necessary to a choice. In every case after the choice of the President, the person having the greatest number of votes of the electors shall be the Vice-President. But if there should remain two or more who have equal votes, the Senate shall choose from them by ballot the Vice-President.

(4) The Congress may determine the time of choosing the electors and the day on which they shall give their votes; which day shall be the same throughout the United States.

(5) No person except a natural born citizen, or a citizen of the United States at the time of the adoption of this Constitution, shall be eligible to the office of President; neither shall any person be eligible to that office who shall not have attained to the age of thirty-five years and been fourteen years a resident with the United States.

(6) In case of the removal of the President from office, or his death, resignation, or inability to discharge the powers and duties of the said office same shall devolve on the Vice-President and the Congress may by law provide for the case of removal, death, resignation, or inability, both of President and Vice-President, declaring what officer shall then act as President, and such officer shall act accordingly, until the disability be removed, or a President shall be elected.

(7) The President shall, at stated times, receive for his services, a compensation, which shall neither be increased nor diminished during the period for which he shall have been elected, and he shall not receive within that period any other emolument from the United States, or any of them.

# Appendix II

## Relevant Part from the Constitution of Finland

*Chapter I.* **General Provisions**

**Article 1.** Finland is a sovereign Republic, its Constitution being established by this constitution Act and by other Constitutional Laws.

**Article 2.** The sovereign power in Finland rests with the people, represented by their delegates assembled in Parliament.

Legislative power shall be exercised by Parliament in conjunction with the President of the Republic.

The supreme executive power is vested in the President of the Republic. In addition to the President there shall be for the general government of the State a council of State consisting of a Prime Minister and the necessary number of Ministers.

The judicial power shall be exercised by independent tribunals and, in the final instance, by the Supreme Court and the Supreme Administrative Court.

*Chapter IV.* **Government and Administration**

**Article 23.** The President of the Republic shall be elected by the people of Finland from among the natural born citizens of Finland. His term office shall be six years.

The election of the President shall be performed by three hundred Presidential Electors. In choosing these electors, the regulations in force for elections to Parliament shall be observed in respect to suffrage and eligibility and, in so far as applicable, also to the mode of election, the procedure of voting and the designation of deputy electors.

The choosing of the electors shall take place on the fifteenth and sixteenth of January; and on the fifteenth of February following, the elector shall assemble under the chairmanship of the Prime Minister to elect the President. The vote shall be by secret ballot. If a candidate obtains more than half of the votes cast, he shall be declared elected; otherwise a new ballot shall be taken immediately, and if no candidate obtains an absolute majority this time, another ballot shall be taken the two candidates who obtained the highest number of votes on the second count. In case of a tie the decision shall be by lot.

If a Member of Parliament is elected President, his mandate as a Member shall cease. A state official who is elected President shall be regarded as having resigned his office.

If a day fixed in Paragraph 3 of this Article or elsewhere in this Constitution Act falls upon a Sunday or a public holiday, the nearest workday following shall be substitute for it.

**Article 26.** For the exercise of his functions the President shall receive an annual emolument, the amount of which shall be fixed by law, and which shall be neither increased nor diminished during his term of office.

**Article 27.** The President shall have the power to summon Parliament to an extraordinary session, to issue orders for elections to Parliament, to open and close the sessions of Parliament, to order new elections, and to dissolve Parliament.

**Article 28.** In cases not otherwise provided for in this present Constitution Act and where such a right has not been vested in the Council of State, the President shall have the right to issue decrees upon matters which have heretofore been regulated by administrative provisions, as well as decrees regulating the execution of laws, the administration of State property, and the organisation and operation of administrative services and public institutions. Decrees shall contain no provision implying a modification of a law.

The procedure for the issue and publication of decrees shall be same as provided in Article 20, Paragraph 2, in respect of laws.

# Appendix III

# Relevant Part from the Constitution of French Republic (France)

Title II *The President of Republic*

**Article 6.** The President of the Republic shall see that the Constitution's respected. He shall ensure, by the arbitration, the regular functioning of the public powers, as well as the continuity of the State.

He shali be the guarantor of national independence of the integrity of the territory, and of respect for Community agreements and for treaties.

**Article 6.** The President of the Republic shall be elected for seven years by direct universal suffrage.

The Procedures implementing the present article shall be determined by an organic law.

**Article 7.** The President of the Republic shall be elected by an absolute majority of the votes caste. If this is not obtained on the first ballots, there shall be a second ballot on the second Sunday following. Only the two candidates who have received the greatest number of votes on the first ballot shall present themselves, taking into account the possible withdrawal of more favoured candidates.

The voting shall be opened upon summons by the Government.

The election of the new President shall take place twenty days at least and fifty days at the most before the expiration of the powers of the President in office.

In the event of a vacancy in the Presidency of the Republic, for any cause whatsoever, or in case of prevention of implement officially noted by the Constitutional Council; to which the matter has been referred by the Government and which shall rule by an absolute majority of its members, the functions of the President of the Republic, with the exception of those provided for by Articles 11 and 12, below, shall be temporarily exercised by the President of the Senate and, if the latter is in his turn prevented or implemented in the exercise of these functions, by the Government.

In case of a vacancy or when the prevention is declared definitive by the Constitutional Council, the voting for the election of a new President shall take place, except in case of *force majeure* officially noted by the Constitutional Council, twenty days at least and thirty five days at the most after the beginning of the vacancy or the declaration of the definitive character of the prevention.

There may be no application of either Articles 49 and 50 or of Article 89 of the Constitution during the vacancy of the Presidency of the definitive character of the impediment of the President of the Republic and the election of his successor.

**Article 8.** The President of the Republic shall appoint the Premier. He shall terminate the functions of the Premier when the latter presents the resignation of the Government.

On the recommendations of the Premier, he shall appointment the other members of the Government and shall terminate their functions.

**Article 9.** The President of the Republic shall preside over the Council of Ministers.

**Article 16.** When the institutions of the Republic, the independence of the nation, the integrity of its territory of the fulfilment of its international commitments are threatened in a grave and immediate manner and the regular functioning of the constitutional public powers is interrupted, the President of the Republic shall take the measures required by these circumstances, after official consultation with the Constitutional Council.

He shall inform the nation of these measures in a message.

These measures must be promoted by the desire to ensure to

the constitutional public powers, in the shortest possible time, the means of accomplishing their mission. The Constitutional Council shall be consulted with regard to such measures.

Parliament shall meet by right.

The National Assembly may not be dissolved during the exercise of exceptional powers.

**Article 19.** The acts of the President of the Republic, other than those provided for under Articles 8 [first paragraph], 11, 12, 16, 18, 54, 56 and 61 shall be countersigned by the Premier, and should circumstances so require, by the appropriate Ministers.

# Appendix IV

# Relevant Part from the Constitution of Sri Lanka

*Chapter VII. President of The Republic*

**Article**

**19. Head of State**

There shall be President of the Republic of Sri Lanka who is the Head of the State.

**Article**

**20. Head of Executive & Commander-in-Chief**

The President is the Head of the Executive and the Commander-in-Chief to the Armed Forces.

**Article**

**26. President's term of office**

(*i*) Subject to the provisions of sub-section (2) of this section, the President holds office for a period of four years:

Provided that, notwithstanding the expiration of this period, the President shall remain in office until the next President assumes office.

(*ii*) The office of the President of the Republic of Sri Lanka becomes vacant:

(a) upon the death of the President;

(b) on the President resigning his office by a writing addressed to the Prime Minister;

(c) on the determination by the Prime Minister that the President is incapable of performing the functions of his office by reason of mental or physical infirmity;

(d) on the National State Assembly passing a resolution of no-confidence against the President proposed by the Prime Minister;

(e) on the National State Assembly passing by at least two-thirds of the whole numbers of the National State Assembly(including those not present) voting in its favour a resolution of no confidence against the President, introduced by any Member by a written notice, addressed to the Speaker signed by such Member and by at least half the total number of Members of the National State Assembly.

**Article**

**27. President to act on advice**

(*i*) The President shall always except as otherwise provided by the Constitution, act on the advice of the Prime Minister, or of such other Minister to whom the Prime Minister may have given authority to advise the President on any particular function assigned to that Minister.

(*ii*) No institution administering justice and likewise no other institution, person or authority shall have the power or jurisdiction to inquire into, pronounce upon or in any manner call in question any act or omission on the part of the President on the ground that the provisions of sub section (1) of this section have not been complied with.

# Appendix V

# Statewise Membership of the Constituent Assembly of India As on 31st December 1947

| Provinces – 229 | | | | | |
|---|---|---|---|---|---|
| | | No. of Members | | | No. of Members |
| 1. | Madras | 49 | 7. | C.P. and Berar | 17 |
| 2. | Bombay | 21 | 8. | Assam | 8 |
| 3. | West Bengal | 19 | 9. | Orissa | 9 |
| 4. | United Provinces | 55 | 10. | Delhi | 1 |
| 5. | East Panjab | 12 | 11. | Ajmer-Merwara | 1 |
| 6. | Bihar | 36 | 12. | Coorg | 1 |

Indian States – 70

| | | | | | |
|---|---|---|---|---|---|
| 1. | Alwar | 1 | 19. | Tripura, Manipur and Khasi States Group | 1 |
| 2. | Baroda | 3 | | | |
| 3. | Bhopal | 1 | 20. | U.P. States Group | 1 |
| 4. | Bikaner | 1 | 21. | Eastern Rajputana States Group | 3 |
| 5. | Cochin | 1 | | | |
| 6. | Gwalior | 4 | 22. | Central India States Group (including Bundelkhand and Malwa) | 3 |
| 7. | Indore | 1 | | | |
| 8. | Jaipur | 3 | | | |
| 9. | Jodhpur | 2 | 23. | Western India States Group | 4 |
| 10. | Kolhapur | 1 | | | |
| 11. | Kotah | 1 | 24. | Gujrat States Group | 2 |
| 12. | Mayurbhanj | 1 | 25. | Deccan and Madras States Group | 2 |
| 13. | Mysore | 7 | | | |
| 14. | Patiala | 2 | 26. | Panjab States Group | 3 |
| 15. | Rewa | 2 | 27. | Eastern States Group I | 4 |
| 16. | Travancore | 6 | 28. | Eastern States Group II | 3 |
| 17. | Udaipur | 2 | 29. | Residuary States Group | 4 |
| 18. | Sikkim and Cooch Bihar Group | 1 | | | |

Total = 229

# Appendix VI

## Lok Sabha Elections (1952-91) Voting Trends

| Election | Congress[1] | CPI | CPI Marxit | PSP/ KMPP | SSP/ Socialist[2] | Bharatiya Jana Sangh (BJP)[3] | Swatantra Party | Congress (O)[4] | Janata/ Bharatiya Lok Dal | Lok Dal | Total for all India parties other than Congress | Total for others (i.e. Local Regional parties and indepen dents |
|---|---|---|---|---|---|---|---|---|---|---|---|---|
| 1. First: 1952 (Total Seats=498; votes polled=105,944,445[61.7%][5]) | | | | | | | | | | | | |
| (a) Percentage of Seats | 74.44 | 3.27 | ... | ... | ... | 0.61 | ... | ... | ... | ... | 3.88 | 21.68 |
| (b) Percentage of Votes | 45.00 | 3.30 | ... | 5.80 | 10.60 | 3.10 | ... | ... | ... | ... | 10.12 | 14.78 |
| 2 Second: 1957 (Total Seats=494; votes polled=123,461,880[63.7%][5]) | | | | | | | | | | | | |
| (a) Percentage of Seats | 75.10 | 5.47 | ... | 3.85 | ... | 0.80 | ... | ... | ... | ... | 10.12 | 14.78 |
| (b) Percentage of Votes | 47.7 | 88.92 | ... | 10.41 | ... | 5.93 | ... | ... | ... | ... | 25.26 | 26.96 |

*(Contd...)*

*(Contd...)*

| | | | | | | | | | | | | |
|---|---|---|---|---|---|---|---|---|---|---|---|---|
| 3 Third: 1962 (Total Seats=494; votes polled=119,904,315[55.4%][5]) | | | | | | | | | | | | |
| (a) Percentage of Seats | 73.08 | 5.87 | ... | 2.43 | ... | 2.83 | 3.64 | ... | ... | ... | 14.77 | 12.15 |
| (b) Percentage of Votes | 44.73 | 9.94 | ... | 6.81 | 2.70 | 6.44 | 7.90 | ... | ... | ... | 33.79 | 21.48 |
| 4. Fourth: 1967 (Total Seats=520; votes polled=152,724,511[61.3%][5]) | | | | | | | | | | | | |
| (a) Percentage of Seats | 54.42 | 4.42 | 3.66 | 2.50 | 4.42 | 6.73 | 8.46 | ... | ... | ... | 30.19 | 15.39 |
| (b) Percentage of Votes | 40.73 | 5.19 | 4.40 | 3.10 | 4.92 | 9.41 | 8.70 | ... | ... | ... | 35.72 | 23.55 |
| 5. Fifth: 1971 (Total Seats=518; votes polled=151,5361,802[55.3%][5]) | | | | | | | | | | | | |
| a) Percentage of Seats | 67.95 | 4.42 | 4.83 | 0.39 | 0.58 | 4.25 | 1.54 | 3.09 | ... | ... | 19.10 | 12.95 |
| b) Percentage of Votes | 43.70 | 4.73 | 5.12 | 1.04 | 2.42 | 7.40 | 3.10 | 10.42 | ... | ... | 34.23 | 22.07 |
| 6. Sixth: 1977 (Total Seats=542; votes polled=194,263,915[60.5%][5]) | | | | | | | | | | | | |
| (a) Percentage of Seats | 28.41 | 1.29 | 4.06 | ... | ... | ... | ... | 0.55 | 54.43 | ... | 60.33 | 11.26 |
| b) Percentage of Votes | 34.52 | 2.82 | 4.30 | ... | ... | ... | ... | 1.72 | 41.32 | ... | 50.16 | 15.32 |

*(Contd...)*

*(Contd...)*

| | | | | | | | | | | | | |
|---|---|---|---|---|---|---|---|---|---|---|---|---|
| 7. Seventh: 1980 (Total Seats=542; votes polled=202,752,893[57.0%][5]) | | | | | | | | | | | | |
| (a) Percentage of Seats | 66.07 | 2.09 | 6.67 | ... | ... | ... | ... | ... | 6.00 | 7.80 | 22.56 | 11.37 |
| (b) Percentage of Votes | 42.70 | 2.61 | 6.10 | ... | ... | ... | ... | 5.30 | 19.00 | 9.40 | 42.46 | 14.90 |
| 8. Eighth: 1984 (Total Seats=542; votes polled=256,335,983[64.1%][5]) | | | | | | | | | | | | |
| (a) Percentage of Seats | 78.64 | 1.17 | 4.32 | ... | ... | 0.39 | ... | 0.78 | 1.94 | 0.58 | 9.18 | 12.18 |
| (b) Percentage of Votes | 49.10 | 2.75 | 5.88 | ... | ... | 7.75 | ... | 1.52 | 6.89 | 5.98 | 30.77 | 20.13 |
| 9. Nineth: 1989 (Total Seats=543; Contested 529; votes polled=298,310,284[59.6%][5]) | | | | | | | | | | | | |
| (a) Percentage of Seats | 37.02 | 2.10 | 6.11 | ... | ... | 16.41 | ... | 0.19 | 27.10 | ... | 51.91 | 11.07 |
| (b) Percentage of Votes | 39.33 | 2.61 | 6.32 | ... | ... | 11.56 | ... | 0.33 | 17.73 | ... | 38.55 | 22.12 |

*(Contd...)*

| | | | | | | | | | | | | |
|---|---|---|---|---|---|---|---|---|---|---|---|---|
| 10. Tenth: 1991 (Total Seats=543; Contested 537; votes polled=285,881,010[55.9%][5]) | | | | | | | | | | | | |
| (a) Percentage of Seats | 45.69 | 2.63 | 6.56 | ... | ... | 22.47 | ... | ... | ... | ... | 43.81 | 10.50 |
| (b) Percentage of Votes | 36.6 | 2.5 | 6.1 | ... | ... | 20.0 | ... | ... | ... | ... | 44.3 | 19.1 |

1. Since 1977, the main Congress Party is referred to as the Congress (I) – i.e., "Indira". The (I) was dropped in 1984.
2. The figures for the 1952 and 1962 elections relate to the Socialist Party, while for the other years they relate to the SSP.
3. The Bharatiya Jana Sangh merged with Janata Party in 1977 but was revived again under the name of Bharatiya Party (BJP) in 1980.
4. The Congress (O) (or 'Organisation') has fragmented into many parties – like the Congress (U), (J), (S) and (B) – since the 1977 election. (Figures for 1989 are of Congress (S) Party).
5. The figures in square brackets indicate the number of votes as a percentage of the total electorate.

*Sources* : V. B. Singh and Shankar Bose, Elections in India: Data Handbook on Lok Sabha Elections 1952-85, 2nd ed., Sage Publications, New Delhi, 1986, and for 1989 elections, A Computerised Analysis for the Press Information Bureau, Government of India. For the tenth general elections, V. B. Singh, Elections in India Data Handbook on Lok Sabha Election 1986-1991, Vol. 2, Sage Publications, New Delhi.

# Index

## M



## N



## O



## P



## Q



## R



## S